LEADING THE LITTLE ONES
TO CHRIST

PRAYER

O JESUS, Who hast loved us unto the ineffable excess of the Eucharist, fire us with an ardent zeal to procure Thy glory by worthily preparing these children, who for the first time are to approach Thy holy table.

O Eucharistic Heart of Jesus, preserve these young souls from evil; strengthen their faith; increase their love; and adorn them with all the virtues which render them worthy to receive Thee. Amen.

May St. John the Baptist, herald of the Messiah, prepare the way for Jesus to enter the hearts of these children.

May St. Tarsicius protect the children, First Communicants.

An indulgence of 500 days is granted to the faithful who devote themselves for at least half an hour to the instruction of children preparing for First Holy Communion. An additional indulgence of 500 days is granted to them if they recite the above prayer.

(Sacred Penitentiary, April 16, 1936)

Prayer for Those Preparing First Communicants.
Translation from Breen's Indulgenced Prayers.

LEADING THE LITTLE ONES TO CHRIST

*An Aid to Catechists of the
First-Communion Class*

Adapted from Gruber-Gatterer
E l e m e n t a r k a t e c h e s e n

By
REV. GEORGE M. DENNERLE

Introduction by
REV. JOSEPH J. BAIERL, S.T.D.
St. Bernard's Seminary, Rochester, N. Y.

ST. AUGUSTINE ACADEMY PRESS
HOMER GLEN, ILLINOIS

Nihil obstat:
    JOHN R. HAGAN,
        Censor deputatus

Imprimatur:
    ✠ JOSEPHUS SCHREMBS,
        Episcopus Clevelandensis

February 1, 1932

ISBN: 978-1-64051-123-1

WAR FORMAT

Departures from the usual Bruce style in
the format of this book are the result of
necessary war conservation of materials
and labor. In every respect, however, the
book is complete and unabridged.

CONTENTS

Page

UNIT EIGHT

UNIT NINE

UNIT TEN

UNIT ELEVEN

INTRODUCTION

If teaching in general is a praiseworthy function, the office of enlightening and training youth in Christian faith and practice is infinitely more noble and laudable, since it is concerned with the most exalted truths, whose value transcends the limits of time and space and whose power for weal or woe reaches into eternity. St. John Chrysostom says: "He who is apt at training the hearts of children surpasses by far the best painter, the best sculptor, indeed any artist or scientist." The teaching of religion and morality is always an arduous task, but its difficulties increase when the children who are to be trained are very young and immature. Elementary catechization is for many teachers a real cross, which they seek to transfer to the shoulders of others whenever feasible. Perhaps one of the chief reasons is the dearth of practical helps for this type of education.

We owe a debt of gratitude to Father M. Gatterer, S.J., of the University of Innsbruck, for having placed at our disposal a booklet which ought to lighten this burden to a considerable degree. In 1922 Father Gatterer republished the excellent

Elementarkatechesen[1] of Augustine Gruber, with an appendix of his own in which he gives a brief theory of elementary catechization and some practical examples for the Eucharistic training of children of the first school year.

Augustine Gruber was born at Vienna in 1763. He was appointed Bishop of Laibach in 1816, and was Archbishop of Salzburg in Austria from 1828 to his death in 1835. During the years 1828, 1829, and 1830 he lectured to his clerics on St. Augustine's famous work, *De catechizandis rudibus*, illustrating these lectures with appropriate practical demonstrations which later on were published. Gruber broke completely with the rationalistic spirit in the sphere of catechetics, which still held sway in his day. The catechist, he insisted, is not a Socrates who evokes truths from the minds of his pupils, but rather God's messenger who speaks in the name of God and who imparts to his wards the divinely revealed truths with great clarity and warmth and who demands from them a firm, active, and living faith. He intended after the publication of his lectures on St. Augustine's volume

---

[1]Augustine Gruber's *Elementarkatechesen* neu herausgegeben und mit einer Theorie der Elementarkatechese vermehrt von Michael Gatterer, S.J. (Innsbruck: Felix Rauch, 1922).

to edit some practical instructions in the spirit of this great Church Father for use in the various grades of the grammar school. However, only his *Elementarkatechesen,* that is, catechetical sketches for the children of the primary grade, and some explanations of the small Catechism appeared in print. He was unable to complete his exposition of the large Catechism.

Gruber's *Elementarkatechesen* are distinguished by two qualities, namely, warmth of presentation and their practical tendency, which very few catechists have been able to match, and much less to excel. He aimed primarily at influencing the heart and the will of the little ones; he sought to enlighten their understanding and to strengthen their memory only insofar as was necessary to realize his primary and real purpose as a catechist of immature minds. To be sure, he always gave his pupils the whole truth, but he was satisfied to explain the truth only insofar as was required to influence their hearts. Even in the matter of repetitions he was solicitous in the first place not about the retention of the Biblical truths, but rather about deepening the impression of those truths in the feelings and in the will. Hence the fervor and the *warmth* of his presentation, its power to awaken the religious emotions in the child's heart. To this end he employs a means which is very simple and yet difficult of application; namely, the manifestation of his own feelings. He seeks to impart the warmth and fervor of his own emotional life to the hearts of his pupils. Everyone knows how efficacious this means is, not merely in the case of grownups but especially for little children. Instinctively the child's heart endeavors to imitate the feelings which it sees reflected in the eye and in the countenance of the catechist, in the tone of his voice and in his very language. If the catechist's heart is gripped with enthusiasm for the ideals of religion, this inward fire will soon break forth and set aglow the hearts of the children. When the heart is warm with true pathos, there is no need of a long discourse. Gruber had this psychological fact of experience in mind, for instance, in the instruction on God, the Creator of all things, where he repeatedly uses the simple exclamation: "O! the good, the mighty God," and in the recapitulation: "God made everything, everything!" Again, when speaking of the sin of our first parents, he exclaims: "Woe, woe to poor disobedient man!" He utilizes even the repetitions in a way that cannot but warm the hearts of the little ones: "See, children, how good God was to Adam and Eve; how many good things He gave to them! He gave them a body with eyes, ears, mouth, hands, and feet; He gave them a soul, which made them alive, made them see with their eyes, hear with their ears. . . . He placed them in a very beautiful garden, where they had indeed to work, but the work was easy. And He gave them many, many other good things."

This means is simple, but not easy, for it pre-supposes the persistent cultivation of the inner life. Only on that condition will the heart of the cate-chist be set afire again and again in the face of these oft-repeated truths; only on that presupposition will the catechist be able, without much effort, to put himself, or to express it more correctly, to pray himself, into the disposition of heart required by the circumstances.

To mention only a few more of the merits that characterize Gruber's *Elementarkatechesen:* In con-trast with many catechists Gruber is silent on many topics which could be made intelligible to children of the first grade only with difficulty and which, on the other hand, have no significance, or at least very little, for the practical purposes of the cate-chist; for instance, the creation of the world in six days, the nudity of our first parents; he describes God, not as forming, but simply as making the human body out of the slime of the earth; in the lesson on the sin of our first parents he does not speak of an apple, but calls it a fruit in harmony with the Biblical account. On the other hand, however, he makes mention of the sacred duty of labor, since it is of practical significance even for little children. He does not mutilate the doctrines which he presents to the children in order to make them intelligible, rather he offers them in their purity and entirety. Hence, despite their simplicity and childlike tone, his instructions are not superficial, but deep.

Gruber's catechetical expositions indeed manifest certain *defects,* which we do not wish to gloss over. For example, his sentences are sometimes too long, his questions sometimes incomplete, and there are some exegetical inaccuracies; the instructions on the miracles and the passion of Jesus are not elaborated as methodically and fully as one might desire. But the most serious defect is, perhaps, his total silence regarding the Blessed Sacrament, which he seeks to justify by appealing to the example of the Fathers of the Church when instructing the catechumens. It is indeed surprising that Augustine Gruber did not seem to realize the weakness of this reasoning; for in Christian antiquity the *disciplina arcani* was in vogue, which now no longer obtains. Moreover, the early Christian catechumens were unbaptized, whereas now we are dealing with baptized children, who have not only the right but also the duty to receive the Blessed Sacrament when they have arrived at the age of discretion (cf. *Codex jur. can.*, c. 854, 3, 5, and c. 88, 3).

Father Gatterer calls attention to these defects in his Preface to the new edition of Gruber's *Elementarkatechesen* and offers some practical suggestions in the Appendix to this same volume as to ways and means of overcoming these defects, especially regarding the Holy Eucharist, in order that Gruber's instructions may meet the needs of our own times. He points out that the *primary task* of the catechist is to stir up in the hearts of the little ones a great devotion to the Blessed Sacrament and to prepare them as soon as possible for their First Holy Communion. The best means to accomplish this is to fill their hearts with an ardent *love of Christ,* the Divine Friend of children. Truly a sweet and easy task for the catechist who really loves Christ! For where are there hearts more responsive to the love of the Savior than the hearts of little children, who as yet know little of the power of the passions rebelling against the spirit of Divine Love? If the catechist succeeds in accomplishing this *second* task, he has at the same time fulfilled the major part of his primary task; for once the love of the Savior vitalizes the hearts of the little ones, a great devotion to the Blessed Sacrament will spring up in their hearts just as soon as they become conscious of the Real Presence of Jesus in the Holy Eucharist.

But the love of Christ must be a *practical love,* which proves itself by a loyal obedience to God's commandments and especially by generous deeds of *love toward one's neighbor* for the love of God. Moreover, since "Christ dwells by faith in our hearts" (Eph. 3, 17), the catechist must endeavor with apostolic zeal to cultivate in the little ones a deep *faith* in the Savior and His revelation, but particularly in His charity "which surpasseth all knowledge." Finally, since the test of true love consists in the faithful observance of the commandments, a difficult task for the proud and selfish heart of man, the catechist must bend all his efforts to arm and fortify the young hearts with a great *trust* in God.

In a word, our instructions must be *Christocentric* from start to finish after the example of the Apostles and especially of the great St. Paul. We must accustom ourselves to view and to treat all things *sub lumine Christi,* in the light that shines in the Sacred Heart of Jesus Christ. Such was the pedagogy of the Divine Wisdom, which aimed to lead men to the love of the invisible God by means of the visible manifestation of God; that is, by the Incarnation of the Son of God. That is true pedagogy of religion and morality, particularly if the catechist presents to the little ones Christ seated on the lap of His Mother, if he leads them to Jesus by the hand of Mary.

Hence, Father Gatterer begins his talks to the little ones by revealing to them *Jesus, the Divine Friend of children*. He shows them in the second lesson the sympathetic and eternal love of Jesus by speaking to them of the *Messengers of the Divine Friend*. Then they are prepared for the touching instructions of Gruber. He suggests that the catechist give to his instructions a *Eucharistic coloring by frequent allusions to the Blessed Sacrament*, by asking the children to make *personal observations* of the facts which they see and hear in the church, especially at the altar and the Communion rail, by adding from time to time *short stories illustrating various circumstances connected with First Holy Communion,* and by making a generous use of *colored pictures.*[2] Father Gatterer also calls attention to the excellent suggestions of Father J. Minnichthaler, of Vienna, which may be utilized with

---

[2] Cf. M. Gatterer, S.J., *Katechetik* (Innsbruck: Felix Rauch, 1931), 4th edition, pp. 143–149.

great profit during the first year in enlightening and training the little ones as regards Holy Mass.

But all this valuable material is in German and, therefore, inaccessible to the average English-speaking catechist. We are indebted to Father George Dennerle of the Cleveland diocese first, for having given us a free translation and adaptation of Gruber's *Elementarkatechesen,* and secondly, for having cleverly worked into the original text the practical suggestions of Fathers Gatterer and Minnichthaler together with many additions of his own. Consequently, his work is in many respects new, while at the same time holding fast to what is best in traditional catechization. Father Dennerle has been using his book for a considerable time in the school to which he was attached as assistant pastor, thus testing theory by practice, and has been ably assisted by the Sisters of Notre Dame of the Cleveland diocese, who have offered some valuable suggestions and revisions in the matter of planning the course for schoolroom use and especially in the "Activities" added to the lessons. We feel confident that Father Dennerle's book makes a real contribution to our ever-growing catechetical literature. Whoever uses this book systematically throughout the first school year will discover that only a few heart-to-heart talks will be necessary to prepare the little ones more directly for their great day of days, their First Holy Communion.

May the blessing of the Great Catechist, the Friend of little children, accompany this volume on its journey for the greater honor of God and the salvation of souls.

JOSEPH J. BAIERL

St. Bernard's Seminary,
Rochester, N. Y.

Lesson	Doctrine	Application
1	Jesus Loves Children	Visiting Eucharistic Jesus
2	The Disciples of Jesus	Pope, Bishop, Priests
3	Creation	Story — St. Francis
4	God's Goodness to Creatures	God's Daily Visit at Mass
5	Obedience to God	Story — Blessed Julie
6	The Sin of Adam and Eve	My Sins — Confessing Them
7	Punishment of Sin	Food of Death—Food of Life
8	Original Sin—Effects on Us	Story — Mary's Temptation
9	The Annunciation	Holiness and Obedience
10	The Nativity	The Christmas Crib
11	Holy Mass	Assisting at Mass
12	The Three Wise Men	Their Gifts — Tabernacle Light
13	Simeon and Anna	Obedience to God's Voice Holy Communion — St. Gerard
14	Jesus at Twelve	Fourth Commandment
15	Jesus is Baptized	Blessed Trinity — Baptism
16	Miracles of Jesus	Reverence Toward Jesus
17	Love of God	First Three Commandments
18	Love of Neighbor	Last Seven Commandments

PLAN

Lesson	Religious Practice	Prayer	Activity
1	Folding Hands at Prayer	Sign of the Cross	Constructing a Church
2	Greeting Jesus and His Messengers		Sand Table — Mission Unit
3	Simple Genuflection	Our Father I	Constructing an Altar
4	Behavior in Church	Our Father II	
5		Our Father III	Sand Table — Creation
6	Striking the Breast	Contrition	
7	Repetition	Morning Prayers	
8		Repetition	Religion Booklet — Pictures
9	Small Sign of the Cross	Hail Mary I	Constructing Classroom Crib
10	Hymns at the Crib	Hail Mary II	Chores for Jesus' Crib
11			Religion Booklet The Home Altar
12		Act of Faith	Paper Cutting: Star; Camel
13	Thanksgiving after Communion	Act of Hope	Dramatization of Story
14	First Communion Hymns	Act of Love	Activities Around Crib
15	Repetition—Sign of the Cross		Drawing — Shamrock
16	Eucharistic Hymns		Cutting and Pasting Pictures
17	Visiting the Confessional	Confession Prayers	Motto Cards
18	Acts of Kindness		Dramatization — Good Samaritan

Lesson	*Doctrine*	*Application*
19	Immortality of the Soul	Story — Little Nellie
20	Resurrection of the Body	Holy Communion
21	Friends and Enemies of Jesus	Missionary Story
22	First Part of Holy Week	Processions in Honor of Jesus
23	Holy Thursday	Contrition — Holy Eucharist
24	Jesus Suffers for Us	The Crucifix — Sorrow
25	Death and Burial of Jesus	Friday Abstinence
26	The Resurrection of Jesus	Resurrection of Our Bodies
27	The Ascension of Jesus	Story — Tarsicius
28	Descent of the Holy Ghost	The Church
29	Holy Mass	Story — Jesus in the Host
30	Holy Communion	Food of the Soul — Desire
31	Holy Communion: Jesus Comes	Story — Imelda
32	Summary — Apostles' Creed I	
33	Summary — Apostles' Creed II	
34	Summary — Our Father, Hail Mary	
35	General Summary	Love and Obey Triune God

PLAN

Lesson	Religious Practice	Prayer	Activity
19		Holy Commun-ion: Desire	
20	How to Receive Holy Communion		Motto Cards
21	Examination of Conscience	For the Missions	
22	Double Genuflection		Dramatization
23	Little Lenten Pen-ances		
24	Little Lenten Pen-ances	Night Prayers	
25	Veneration of Cru-cifix	Contrition	Sand Table — Stations
26		Communion Prayers	Religion Booklet — Pictures
27		Baptismal Vows	Dramatization — Tarsicius
28	Manner of Receiving Holy Communion		Religion Booklet — Pictures
29	Rules for Reception of Holy Com-munion	Repetition: Communion Prayers	Religion Booklet — Lettering
30	Practice of Above	Repetition of Above	Crayon Drawing
31			Religion Booklet — Picture
32	Repetition	Apostles' Creed I	
33	Repetition	Apostles' Creed II	
34	Repetition	Our Father	
35		Hail Mary	Prayer Booklet: Pictures

UNIT ONE

Content

1. Jesus, the Friend of Children.
2. The Messengers of Jesus.

Objectives

1. To acquire a personal love for Jesus, Friend of children.
2. To become acquainted with persons who represent Christ on earth.
3. To develop an attitude of respect toward Jesus in the Blessed Sacrament and toward the persons who represent Him.
4. To learn how to make the sign of the cross.

Part One

JESUS, THE FRIEND OF CHILDREN

Picture

Devices

The Divine Friend of Children (Schumacher)[1]

Introduction

Children, we shall first say a prayer to the good God. (*The Our Father. The teacher recites the prayer slowly and the children stand in the attitude of prayer.*)

Procedure

I am happy to be with you, children, because I love you very much. Your father and mother love you very much, too. But now I shall tell you about Someone Who loves you much more than I do, even more than your father and mother. That One is the dear Savior, Jesus Christ. You must also love Him. (*Show the picture of Jesus Friend of Children. Let the little ones look at it quietly, then*

---

[1] P. Schumacher, *Religious Wall Pictures*. An excellent set of sixty colored pictures, 31 by 22 in. (Munich, J. Koesel, and F. Pustet; New York, Frederick Pustet.) Another very good set is *Nelson's Bible Wall Pictures*, containing 282 subjects of the Old and New Testaments in colors, 32 by 23 inches (New York, Thomas Nelson and Sons). Other sets of large pictures are published by Father Nell of Effingham, Illinois, and by Father Heeg. On page 306 f., we give an ample list of picture-subjects with their artists, for those who prefer the famous masterpieces.

point to Jesus.) See! That is the dear Jesus — our Savior, Jesus Christ. (*The children should then look up at the teacher.*) I shall now tell you about the dear Jesus, that you may learn to be very good. Pay close attention! Then you will make Jesus very happy. (*The teacher turns to the picture and says: O Divine Jesus, help me to teach Your children well!*)

Presentation

1. (*Tell the story with the aid of the picture.*) One day some pious mothers came to the Savior. (*Point out in the picture.*) Some were carrying their little children in their arms, others were holding them by the hand. (*Show on the picture.*) The bigger children stood at mother's side or held on to mother's dress. (*Show.*) These good mothers said to the Divine Savior: "Dear Jesus, lay Your hands upon our children and bless them." These little ones were not afraid of Jesus. They looked right up into His face. Some of them stretched out their little hands. They wanted Jesus to take them in His arms. (*Show.*) Then the good, great Jesus put His hand on their heads and blessed them. The wee little children He took into His arms. What a dear, kind Savior! See how good He is! See how He loves children!

2. (*Tell the story without the picture.*) Children, now I'll tell you this story again. Listen closely! (*The picture is put aside and the story is repeated in the same words.*) In conclusion, the teacher says: Oh, the good Jesus! How happy those mothers were! And the children too! Their little eyes beamed with joy and their little hearts beat with gladness. How they loved the good Jesus! How happy they were! The bigger children said to the Savior: "Dear, kind Jesus, we will be very good."

Recapitulation

(*Little children are not able to repeat a story in exact narrative form. Hence, the teacher points to the various persons in the picture and asks questions as follows.*) Who is this? (Yes, the dear, good Jesus.) And who are these? To Whom did these mothers come? Are they dressed like your mother? (No, these were good Jewish mothers.) Now look at the children. How is the mother taking this child to Jesus? (In her arms.) And this one? (She is leading it by the hand.) And these bigger children? (They are standing alongside of mother, and this one is holding on to its mother's dress.)

These good mothers love their children very much and they want Jesus to bless their little ones. See! The mothers are looking up into Jesus' face.

They are saying something to Him. Do you know what they are saying? What did Jesus do then? That made the children happy. They loved the Savior. They liked to be with Him. Why does that one little child want to go to Jesus' arms?

Children, if you could have been there with those little ones, you would have been very happy. The dear, Divine Savior would have put His hand on you. He would have blessed you, too, and made you good. Jesus, the Savior, loves you. You ought to love Him also. You should try to make the good Savior happy, too.

Doctrinal — Jesus' Presence in the Holy Eucharist

Application   Children, if the dear Jesus were only here now, how lovely that would be! How happy you would feel! But listen! Jesus, the Friend of children, is not far from here now. He is very near. He is looking at you this very minute. He loves you, too. Do you know where He is? Yes, He is in the church, in a little golden house on the altar. After a little while, I shall take you for a visit to the great Jesus. You cannot see Him. But He sees you and will bless you, because He loves you very much. O dear Savior Jesus, how much You love my children!

(*Repeat in question form.*) Children, if Jesus

were here, how would we feel? Where is the good Savior? What is the great Jesus doing this very minute? Do you see the dear Jesus? Dear Jesus loves you. What should you do?

Liturgical and Practical — Visit to Jesus. Behavior in Church

The mothers brought their children to the Savior. Your mothers take you to church, too, or they send you to church. Your good mothers! Go gladly to church when they send you. Ask your father and mother to take you to church when they go. Jesus, our God, is waiting for you in the church. The good Savior!

When you are in church visiting Jesus, you must be like the Jewish children in the picture. Look up toward the altar, to the dear Jesus, just as that little girl is doing. Fold your hands nicely like that little boy. Love Jesus like that wee little child that stretches out its hands to Him. Say to the Savior (*have the children stand*): "O Jesus, I Love You!" (*Repeat three times.*) That is what you should say when you are in church. Just say it quietly to yourself.

(*Repeat in question form.*) Where is the dear Jesus? What should we be happy to do? When your mother sends you to church, you should be happy

to go. When she goes to church, you should be glad
to go with her. Where should you look when you
are in church? How should you fold your hands?
I shall tell you more about that in just a moment.
What should you say to Jesus?

Yes, love the Savior. Love Him dearly. Love
Jesus even more than you love your father and
mother. You must try to make Him happy, too.
At home, in church, and in school, you must try to
please Jesus.

Folding Hands at Prayer

*Religious
Practice*

Now stand up, children. Fold your hands as you
see me doing. (*Fold hands, finger to finger, right
thumb crossed over the left thumb, in almost verti-
cal position before the breast.*) The dear Jesus is
glad when you fold your hands nicely like this.
Watch closely and do just as I am doing. Then
you will make Jesus glad. (*The practice is concluded
with the following remarks.*) Children, now Jesus
is happy with you. Say this little prayer with me:
"Dear Jesus, we love You. We will please You."
(*Repeat.*)

Sign of the Cross

Prayer

Whenever we pray, we begin by making the sign
of the cross. Would you like to learn how to make

the sign of the cross? Then watch me closely. (*Show the children how to make it, using, of course, your left hand and touching your right shoulder first. Teach the action first without the words.*) Now children, make the sign of the cross with me. But first hold up your right hand. That is the hand with which you make the sign of the cross. The left hand is placed under the breast. With the fingers of your right hand touch your forehead, then your breast just above the left hand, then your left shoulder, and finally your right shoulder. (*Practice with the children several times. Call upon individuals to do it. Now you are ready to teach the words with the action. At the forehead — "In the name of the Father"; at the breast — "and of the Son"; at the left shoulder — "and of the Holy"; at the right shoulder — "Ghost. Amen."*) Children, Jesus is pleased when you make the sign of the cross. He loves the cross. You should love it, too. Always make the sign of the cross well.

Constructing a church, such as suggested in *Art Education Through Religion*, Book I[2] would be ***Activity*** a most appropriate and profitable activity for Part One. Along with the construction of the church we

---

[2]*Art Education Through Religion*, Book I, by Mary Gertrude McMunigle (New York: Mentzer, Bush & Co., 1930).

would suggest the making of a reading chart. Guided by the tactful questions of the teacher, the children will most probably venture statements such as the following for the chart:

"We Made a Church."

"The Church is the House of God."

These charts can be used again during the latter part of the year, when the children are able to write, as a means of reviewing. Have the children copy their little stories in their religion booklet.

We would also suggest the making of a large church for the classroom. This can be done by a group of children during their work period. A large carton can be used. A steeple can be cut out of wrapping paper and attached to a stick. This church can be used for the dramatization in Part Two.

Remarks

From the very beginning, we must insist upon the exact performance of religious practices, because the child's own devotion for life and the edification of others depend upon it. The important thing is that the teacher should watch closely that these first practices are done exactly and with devotion.

The teacher should not always speak to the children about the "dear" Jesus. Other adjectives which denote the majesty and greatness of God should also be used. This will foster reverence toward God.

The constructive instinct of the child may be made a means of mental growth in religious knowledge through the "Activities." Constructing, dramatizing, and drawing unquestionably sustain interest which is a vital element in all learning. However, all such activity in the classroom should be controlled. It is to be used as a means of establishing and fixing the doctrines or practices taught.

Part Two

THE MESSENGERS OF JESUS

Pictures

Devices

The Divine Friend of Children (Schumacher)
The Reigning Pope
The Local Bishop

Introduction

Children, you ought to love the Divine Savior because He loves you so much. The dear Jesus loves children very, very much. That is why He is *Procedure* called the Divine Friend of children. Who still remembers something about the Divine Friend of children?

Today, I shall tell you more about Him. Pay close attention and you will make Jesus happy. "O Divine Friend of children, bless these children that they may pay attention and ever love You more and more."

Presentation

(Tell the story with the aid of the picture.)

Do you see anyone else in the picture besides Jesus, the children, and their mothers? Wherever Jesus went these men went along with Him. They were called disciples. How many can you see in the picture? The others are farther back and you cannot see them. These men made angry faces when the mothers came to Jesus with their children. See! One of them is still making an angry face. *(Point out in the picture.)* The disciples said to the mothers: "Go away! Let the Savior rest now. He is tired." When Jesus heard this, He said to the disciples: "No, let the children come to Me. Do not keep them away. The kingdom of heaven is for children." Our Lord wants to have the children with Him, even though He is tired. O dear, good Jesus, how You love little children!

The disciples loved Jesus very much. Because they loved Him so much and because Jesus was tired, they made angry faces at the mothers and wanted to send them away. But when they saw how the Savior loved the children, they stopped making angry faces and began to love these children too. See! That disciple is not making an angry face any more. *(Point out in the picture.)* After a while, the disciple with the white beard also smiled kindly at the children. They were good disciples.

Later on, Jesus said to the disciples: "My disciples, you must love the children just as you love Me." The disciples remembered what Jesus said, and after that they always loved children. Just before Jesus went away to heaven, He sent His disciples into the whole world as His messengers. He sent them to the children, too. The disciples were His messengers. These messengers of God were then very kind to the children. They taught them and blessed them just as the Savior did, and made them good. They were good disciples, these messengers of the Savior, weren't they? The children, too, were glad to go to these messengers of God, and by doing so they became better and better children. O good Savior, I thank You because You sent such messengers to the children!

Recapitulation

Now, children, I shall tell you the story again. What do you call these men? (*Point out in the picture.*) Where are the others? The disciples were always with Jesus. They learned their lessons from Him. What kind of face is that disciple making? The others also made angry faces. Why are they making angry faces? What did the disciples say to the mothers? How did the Savior answer them? Oh! the good, kind Jesus! Even though He is tired, the children can come to Him. He takes them into His arms, as your Father and Mother do to you. He puts His hand on their head and blesses them. The dear Jesus also loves you that much. You should love Him too.

Why did the disciples make angry faces at the mothers? Did they stop making angry faces when Jesus told them He loved the children? What did Jesus tell the disciples to do? What did He say to them? Did the disciples do what Jesus said? How did they show that they loved the little children too? What else did they do? They were good disciples. They loved the children and the children loved them.

Application Children, if these messengers of the Savior were here now, they would love you very much; and you would be very happy, I know. This is what you would say to them: "Dear disciples, tell us about the good Jesus. Bless us and make us good."

But listen! The great Jesus has really sent us such messengers. Do you know who they are? These messengers of the Savior are the pope and the bishop. (*Here pictures of the reigning pope and the local bishop may be shown.*) Our good bishop sends out the priests and sisters and other Catholics who teach religion. That means they teach about God. The priests and sisters are the messengers of God. (*Repeat.*) So are those Catholic people who teach religion. I am the Savior's messenger. I shall tell you about the Savior, and bless you (*if the catechist is a priest*), and help to make you good. Children, I am very happy to do this. That is why I do not make an angry face when I come to you. I love you very much. Every day the Savior says to me at Mass and Holy Communion: "My dear messenger, love My children! What you do for them, you do for Me." That is why I love you.

Children, who are the messengers of the Savior? The disciples, did you say? Yes, but they are dead. Who are the Savior's messengers now? (*Repeat. This point is especially important.*) Whom does the bishop send to you? Yes, the priests are the special messengers of God. The good God says to the priest every day: "Love My children, love them very much." That is why the priest likes to come to you.

But you must be glad, too, to come to the Savior's messengers. You should be happy to see the priest and to listen to what he tells you in church and in school. You should be glad to go to school to the sister. When I speak to you, you must look up at me just as the children looked up at the Savior. You must listen carefully, too, just as the children listened to the words of Jesus. Obey me also as those children obeyed Jesus. Then you will make the Savior happy, and He will love you more and more. Every day you will become better and better children.

(*Repeat by means of questions.*) Children, wouldn't we be happy if the disciples of our Lord Jesus were here? What would you say to them? Doesn't the dear Jesus love you as much as He loved the Jewish children? Surely He does. Who are the messengers of the great Jesus now? Who else? Yes, I am one of the Divine Savior's messengers. I speak to you about Jesus. I like to do it, because I love you. When does the dear Jesus tell me to love you and speak to you?

Children, when you go to church the Lord Jesus always says something to you. Do you know what He says? "Dear child," He whispers, "you must love your priests and sisters. I have sent them to you as My messengers. You must pay attention when they speak to you. You must do as they say. You must pray for them." A good little boy and girl will always remember this: LOVE WHAT THE MESSENGERS OF GOD TEACH YOU. (*Repeat two or three times.*) You will do that, children, will you not? Stand up now, fold your hands, and say after me: "Dear Jesus, we love You. We love Your priests and sisters too. We will pay close attention to them and will do what they ask us to do."

(*If the catechist is a priest, he may bless the children after the example of the Savior, using the formula "Benedictio Dei" and repeating it in English.*)

Greeting to Jesus in the Blessed Sacrament and to His Messengers

Now children, this is the way we show our love for Jesus, the Divine Friend of children, and for His messengers. Where does holy Jesus stay all day and night? The church is Jesus' house. When you pass by the house of one of your little friends, what do you do? We should greet Jesus, too, when we pass by His house. This is how we do it. When a little boy passes by a Catholic church, he should tip his cap and say, "Jesus, I love You." (*Have several of the boys dramatize.*) Now the little girls do something else. They bow their head just a little (*like this*), and say with hearts full of love, "Jesus, I love You." (*Have several dramatize this.*) When the little boys meet one of the messengers of Jesus, they should tip their cap and say with a smile, "Good morning, Father!" or "Good afternoon, Father!" or "Good morning, Sister!" (*Have several dramatize.*)

Religious Practice

Remember this, dear children. Never pass good, kind Jesus or His messengers without greeting them.

Culminating Activity
Construct a mission unit on the sand table. A small church, as in Part One; a school, built the same as the church except for the steeple; cut-outs of priests, sisters, and children — are the items suggested for this Mission Unit. Model a cross and have the children select a suitable place for it in the group. Finish the reading chart with the following statements:

Boys should tip their caps when they pass God's house.

They should say, "Jesus, I love You."

The girls bow their heads when they pass God's house.

They say, "Jesus, I love You."

Remarks
The guiding thought of the catechist throughout should be: The Savior has so loved children that He sent His own messengers who are to teach them, bless them, and make them good and happy. A more detailed explanation of "messengers of God" is not given. Definitions are too difficult for small children. By speaking of the disciples as the messengers of God or as the messengers of Jesus, the child is sufficiently enabled to conclude for itself that the catechist is sent by the Savior.

In the matter of repetition, naturally the more important truths should be more often repeated. The teacher should not be too strictly bound to a set plan. It is much more important that the objectives be kept constantly in mind.

By the frequent blessing of the priest, the children receive in the first place the benefits of a sacramental. At the same time they learn to understand the priestly blessing and that part of the Mass in which it is used.

UNIT TWO

Content

1. God, the Creator of All Things.
2. God's Goodness toward Us.
3. Our Return of Love: Obedience to God

Objectives

1. To develop an appreciation of God's goodness and of His creation.

2. To develop sentiments of gratitude that will stimulate the spirit of giving God pleasure through obedience.

3. To learn little ways of serving God, such as the genuflection and our greeting to Jesus at the Elevation of the Mass.

4. To learn how to say the "Our Father."

Part One

GOD, THE CREATOR OF ALL THINGS

Pictures

God and His Creation (Schumacher)

St. Francis and the Birds

Devices

Introduction

Procedure

Children, do you still remember Who sent me to you? Whose messenger am I? Today, I shall tell you some of the holy lessons that the good Savior wants me to teach you. Many of these things are about the dear, great God. The Savior Himself is God, you know. He is the Son of God. As God's Son He is always with God. He was with Him at the time when God made the world. After a few moments I shall tell you how God made the world.

Presentation

1. Your parents have surely told you something about God, haven't they? You have often seen them praying to the loving Father in heaven. They

23

have prayed with you, too. Perhaps your mother said the prayer and you prayed it after her. Or perhaps your father and mother have taken you to church. There you saw many people kneeling and praying. Those people who were kneeling and praying were speaking to God. They were asking Him for the things they needed. Or they were thanking Him for the good things He already gave them. Or they were telling Him they would do everything He wanted them to do. Those people asked God to love them, because they are His children and He is their Father.

2. You are still little, my dear children. Some of you may have brothers or sisters at home who are still smaller than you. At one time, they were not here on this earth. At one time, you were not here either. God gave you your father and mother, your brothers and sisters. Now Who gave you your parents? and Who gave you yours? and you?

Even the earth on which we live was not always here. God made it. The beautiful sun, too, which keeps us warm and gives us light, was not always here. God made the sun.

3. (*Tell the story with the picture. Point out details as you progress.*) God made heaven and earth. Just as quickly as He wanted the heavens,

the heavens were made. Then God said again:
"Let there be earth." And there was earth. All
things came just as quickly as God wanted them.
In heaven God made the angels. We shall learn
about them after a little while. God made the land
and the water. He also made the trees and bushes,
the plants and the grass. Above the earth God put
the sun and the moon and the stars. He made the
fishes in the water, the birds in the air, the animals
on the land. He made them all. At last God made
two people: a man and a woman. God called the man
Adam. The woman's name was Eve. Yes, children,
God made all things. He just wished them and they
were made. That is why we say: God created all
things. O good and powerful God!

Recapitulation

Now children, who made heaven? Who made the
earth? Who made the angels in heaven? Who made
the water and the land? The trees, bushes, plants,
and grass? The sun, moon, and stars? The fishes,
birds, and animals? Who made them all? Who made
the first man, Adam? The first woman, Eve? Who
made all things?

Who made you? and you? and you? Who made
all the children in this room? Who made all the

other children on this earth? And the big people
— who made them all? Who created all things?
Oh, the good and powerful God!

Oral Completion Test

1. As quickly as God wished the earth to be, it
was . . .

2. As quickly as God wished the fishes, birds,
and animals to be, they were . . .

Doctrinal — Love of the Creator and all His Creatures. Story of St. Francis of Assisi

Application

Children, now I shall tell you the story of a
great saint who loved God very much and who loved
all the things God made. This saint's name was
Francis. St. Francis loved the flowers and the birds
and the animals that God created. He loved them
so much that he called them his little brothers and
sisters.

One day St. Francis was walking through the
country. Out in the field he spied a flock of birds.
He was very happy when he saw all the beautiful
birds. He went up close to them and called to them.
They were not afraid of him. They did not fly
away, but came close and sat around him on the
ground. There were many different kinds of birds

there — the red-breast, the sparrow, the warbler, the lark, and others.

Then St. Francis preached to them. This is what he said: "My sisters, the little birds, you should always sing a song of love and thanks to God. See how much God does for you! He gives you pretty feathers to keep you warm. He gives you the air to fly in. You do not have to work, yet God gives you food and drink. He gives you the hills and the mountains for your playground, the high trees for your home. Thank the good God for all His love."

When St. Francis stopped preaching, all the little birds flapped their wings and fluttered about his head. Then Francis blessed them with the sign of the cross, and they flew away in every direction. "Love God," St. Francis called after them, "and sing aloud your sweet, heavenly song."

St. Francis was happy when he saw all the beautiful things God had made. So, children, you should be happy when you see all the things God has made. When you think that God made you, be happy. Be happy and thank God, too, when you think of the good father and mother God gave you. Be happy and thank God when you see the sun, moon, and stars, the flowers, the birds and animals that God made for you.

God made all things. He created everything. Oh, the good and great God!

Liturgical and Practical — The Great God Lives in Our Tabernacles

Children, the great God Who made all things does not live far from here. He lives in the church, in that little house on the altar, called the tabernacle. Did you ever notice the door of that little house? Sometimes the priest opens that door. He looks into the house and then quickly kneels down. Someone very great must live in that little house because the priest kneels down that way. Yes, children, the great God Who created all things lives there. Now you know why the priest kneels down when he opens the door of that house, don't you? He kneels down, too, whenever he passes in front of that little house.

The people also kneel down before the tabernacle when they come into the church. Do you know why they kneel down? Who lives there? Yes, the great God Who made all things. Would you like to learn how to kneel down, too?

The Genuflection

Religious Practice   Now children, stand up straight. Fold your hands. Put your right foot back, then let your right knee touch the floor just beside your left heel. Keep your body straight. Then rise right away. Watch how I do it. (*Have one of the brighter children show the class how the genuflection should be made.*)

You call that a genuflection. You should make a genuflection like that before you go into your bench in church and when you go out of your bench. Always make the genuflection nicely. Look straight at the tabernacle and say: "JESUS, I LOVE YOU." The great God smiles when you greet Him devoutly.

The Our Father

Practice the words of the Our Father from the beginning to "Thy will be done on earth as it is in heaven" included. Refer to the picture of "God and His creation" to give the children a setting for their prayer. No detailed explanation is given at this time.   *Prayer*

Construct an altar as suggested in *Art Education Through Religion*, Book II.[1] Besides the individual altars we would suggest having a group construct an altar for the large church. Emphasize the tabernacle on the altar.   *Activity*

---

[1]*Art Education Through Religion*, Book II, by Mary Gertrude McMunigle (New York: Mentzer, Bush & Co., 1930).

Remarks   Notice that the instruction proceeds in a positive
manner. No authority is given for any statements. That
would be useless with children, since they believe your
word. Furthermore, it would be harmful, as nothing
shakes the belief in authority more than the overeager
desire to prove it.

The instruction begins historically. God's entire revelation was made historically. Moreover, the ideas are
not conveyed by means of fixed, determined words.
Strive only to get the idea correctly to the children.
The definite fixing of terms belongs to later instructions. Speak of the power of God without using the
words omnipotent or all-powerful. The correct notion
of God's power is given when you tell the little ones
that "as soon as God wished it, it was there." The
words "made" and "create" are used interchangeably
as expressing the same idea, without going into the explanation of the word "create."

Work on the child's feeling of joy in God. Remind
the child often of God. Combine the thought of God
with the commonplace things of the little one's life.

Part Two

GOD'S GOODNESS TO US

Picture

Devices   Adam and Eve in the Garden of Paradise
(Schumacher)

Introduction

Dear children, in our last lesson we learned of
Procedure   many wonderful things that God created. Who can

name some of the things God made? Today, I shall tell you how God made the first two people and what He did to make them happy.

Presentation

1. God first made Adam. In the beginning Adam's body was not alive. His body had eyes, but they could not see. It had ears, but they could not hear. It had hands and feet, but they could not move. Then God put into Adam's body something that we call the soul. At once his body became alive.

After God had created the first man, He also created the first woman. Her name was Eve. This is how God created Eve. While Adam was in a sound sleep, God took a rib out of his body and built another body around it. Then He put a soul into Eve's body and she became alive.

Who of you has ever seen a dead person? A dead person has eyes. Can these eyes see anything? He has ears. Can these ears hear? He has hands and feet. Can these hands and feet move? Do you know why? There is no soul in a dead body. The soul makes us live.

2. (*Show the picture.*) God was happy when He made Adam and Eve. He wanted to make them happy too. So He placed them in a beautiful garden, where there were many fine trees and many kinds

of fruit. There was also pure, running water in this garden. The air was sweet and pleasant. In this garden, Adam and Eve were going to work, but this work would not be hard for them. God allowed them to eat the fruit of the beautiful trees and the things that grew in the ground. He also commanded the animals to obey Adam and Eve.

See, children, how good God was to Adam and Eve! How happy He made them! He gave them a body with eyes, ears, a mouth, and hands and feet. He gave them a soul which made them living. They could see with their eyes, they could hear with their ears, they could talk and eat with their mouth, they could work with their hands, they could walk and run with their feet. Then God put them into a very beautiful garden. They had to keep this garden neat and clean. But the work was easy, and they did not grow tired at all. God gave them all kinds of good things in this garden.

3. God is just as good to us. He is good to us now. He has been good to us always. We have a body with eyes, ears, mouth, hands, and feet. In this body we have a soul. The soul gives our body life. Yes, and God makes things grow for our food. These things make us happy. God keeps the sun in the heavens to give us light and heat. He gives you children, who are not yet big enough to work hard, good, kind parents to care for you. He gives you

other people, too, who love you and help you. Oh, how good God is to you! How kind He is to all of us!

4. God is also very good to the angels He created. These angels are with Him in heaven. He is very kind to them. They are glad to be with God in heaven. God loves them and makes them happy.

Recapitulation

God is so good to everyone and to everything He has made. How was He to Adam and Eve? He gave them a body. What did that body have? What made the bodies of Adam and Eve living bodies? Now tell me some of the good things God placed in the garden for Adam and Eve to enjoy. God is good to us, too. He gave us a body. What has our body to see with? to hear with? to work with? to walk and run with? What makes our body live? What makes our eyes to see, our ears to hear, our hands to work, our feet to walk and run? Who gave us our soul? Yes, God is very kind to us. He is also very kind to the angels. What does He give them?

Oral Completion Test

1. When God gave Adam and Eve all those good things in the garden, He showed that He . . . . them.

2. All the good things He gives us show that He . . . us too.

Doctrinal

Application

Children, we must love God because He has loved us so much. It would not be right, if we did not love the person who gave us many beautiful things. If someone loves me, I should love him too. If he makes me happy, I should try to make him happy too.

Adam and Eve should have loved God because He loved them so much. They should have pleased God because He gave them so many good things to make them happy. God also loved the angels very much. In return they wanted to love Him. He did so much to make them happy. Can you tell me what they would want to do for Him? Now listen, children! God loves you, each one of you, and He loves me. So we ought to love God. He gives you and me very many things to make us happy. What should we try to do in return?

Every day try to think of how good and kind God is to you. If I tell you by and by how you can please God, what will you try to do? Why will you try to please God? In the next lesson I shall tell you what you must do to please God. But for today, remember that you should often think of how good God is to you. When you get up in the morning, when you eat, when you go to bed at night, in church, and in school, think of this: O GOD, HOW GOOD AND KIND YOU ARE! I WILL LOVE YOU AND PLEASE YOU!

Liturgical and Practical — God's Daily Visit in the Holy Mass

How beautiful was life for Adam and Eve in the garden! God would often come to them toward evening and talk kindly to them, as a father with his children. How happy Adam and Eve were then! But children, we can be just as happy as Adam and Eve. The same God comes to visit us each morning in our church at Holy Mass. He is kind to us, too, just as a father to his children. He speaks to us sweetly and blesses us. He watches over us and helps us.

How happy we should be to go to church when we know that God will come to visit us! How often does God come to pay us this visit? So we ought to be glad to go to church every morning to have God visit us. Is it wrong if we do not go every morning? No! But one day every week we must go to Mass. What day of the week is that?

External Behavior at Mass

Religious Practice

When you go to Mass, God will visit you and you will visit Him. As you come into the church, you first have to greet God. You greet Him by taking holy water as you come into the church and making the sign of the cross. This is the way you take holy water. Dip the tips of the fingers of your right hand in the holy water. Then make the sign of the cross slowly and devoutly. (*Repeat here the practice of making the sign of the cross.*) Then you go to your place in the church. Before you go into your bench, you make a genuflection. Look straight at the tabernacle and say, "JESUS, I LOVE YOU." (*Repeat the practice of the previous lesson.*)

Children, what do you do when your father comes home from work? He smiles when you greet him. That makes him happy. You ought to greet kind, loving Jesus, too, when you come into the church. Always do it well. That pleases Jesus.

During the Mass look up at the altar. God is there. The priest will hold Him up for you to look at. Listen for the little bell. It will tell you when the priest holds up Jesus. What you see looks like a little piece of white bread. We call it the Sacred Host. But it is God. It is Jesus. Say to Him: "MY LORD AND MY GOD!" (*Practice these words.*)

When you are at Mass, children, do not talk or laugh or play. Jesus sees you. Please Him by being good. (*Here the teacher might call attention to any misbehavior noticed in church. Emphasize the motives for correct behavior.*)

The Our Father

"Give us this day . . . as we forgive those who trespass against us." (*Drill and add the preceding.*)   *Prayer*

In this lesson the idea of the soul has not been developed. It would be too difficult for the children to understand any more than that the soul gives life to the body. All further explanation is left for later years when the child's mind has become more matured. Nor has any mention been made of the soul being a likeness of God. This doctrine is too advanced for beginners.   *Remarks*

Guided by the text of Genesis, chapter 2, verse 15 ("And the Lord God took man, and put him into the paradise of pleasure, to dress it, and to keep it"), we have refuted the false notion that work is a punishment of sin, by stating that Adam and Eve had to work in the Garden of Paradise immediately after their creation. Since a part of the punishment of sin consists not in the labor itself, but in its difficulties for us (Genesis 3, 17), we have added the sentence, "without the labor being hard for Adam and Eve." In our instruction we have developed the love of God from the idea of having joy in God.

Part Three

OUR RETURN OF LOVE: OBEDIENCE

Pictures

Devices

The Guardian Angel (Schumacher)
The Bad Angels Driven out of Heaven

Introduction

Procedure

Children, you know that God created you and me and all things. I am sure you like to think of the great God Who made all things. God is very kind and good. How was He to the angels He created? Where were they? There they were happy with God. How was God to Adam and Eve? He made their bodies with eyes, ears, mouth, hands, and feet. But what did He put into their bodies that made them see, hear, talk, work, and walk? They were not dead but alive. Where did God place Adam and Eve? What kind of place was it? What did they have to do in the garden? Was their work hard? What did God give them for food? God gave them power, too, over all the animals. How was God to Adam and Eve?

Surely the angels were very happy with God. They loved Him very much. They wanted to make Him glad. Adam and Eve felt like loving God too,

when they saw how good and kind He was to them.
And because He did so many things to please them,
what should they have done? If they tried to please
Him, that would be a sign that they loved Him.

Now, dear children, I shall tell you how the
angels pleased God.

Presentation

1. The angels did whatever God commanded
them. They obeyed Him like servants. Yes, they
gladly did all things that God told them. In that
way they pleased God. Some other time, I shall tell
you how God sent some of the angels to this earth
to bring messages to people. They were glad to go
on these errands for God and to do whatever else
He commanded. Did your mother ever tell you
anything about the holy Guardian Angel?

(*Show the picture.*) Children, that is one of the
Guardian Angels. It is the Guardian Angel of that
little child. What a beautiful angel! See his beautiful strong wings! How gentle and kind he looks!
He is bending over that child to keep it from harm.
Just think, children, each one of us has his own
dear Guardian Angel to look after him. When we
were born God sent that angel from heaven to
watch over us. God said to him: "Dear Angel, I
want you to take care of little John for Me. Take

very good care of him. Do not let him hurt himself. Do not let him soil his soul. When he dies bring him back to Me that he may live with Us in Our beautiful heaven." So the Guardian Angel stays with us day and night. He goes wherever we go. He watches over us that we may not hurt ourselves. We cannot see him, but he is there. He whispers to us, too, to be good and obedient to God. Some day, we hope, he will take us up to heaven.

Children, I am sorry to say that some of the angels did not always remain obedient to God. Some of them said to themselves: "We do not always want to do what God wishes; we will not serve Him; we will do as we please." That was very wicked of these angels. They were not good angels any longer. They were bad. God could not be pleased with them now. As long as they were obedient, God let them be happy. But when they became disobedient, He drove them out of heaven into a place we call hell. (*Show the picture of the rejection of the bad angels.*) In heaven these angels had been happy. But oh! they were and still are so unhappy and sad in hell. These bad angels we call devils. Oh, if only they had remained good and obedient to God!

2. Listen now to the story of the first people,

Adam and Eve. God was very good to them, as you know. He gave them many good things in the garden. They really loved the good God and were happy with Him. How should they have acted then toward God? How do you think they could have pleased God? How did the angels please God? So Adam and Eve should have pleased God by obeying Him. God is a Lord or King. Everything He created must obey and follow Him. One who really loves God must do what He says.

Now pay close attention! God told Adam and Eve what He wanted them to do. He gave them an easy law. He said to them: "You may eat the fruit of all the trees in this garden, except the fruit of one tree that grows in the middle. You may not eat the fruit of that tree. If you do, you will have to die." Now, how could Adam and Eve show God that they loved Him? They would not be good if they ate that fruit. That would no: please God.

Recapitulation

How do the angels please God and show that they love Him? Tell me some of the things the good angels do to please God. How does our Guardian Angel please God? Did all the angels always

do what God told them to? They were bad angels
then. They did not love God any more. What did
God do to these bad angels?

How can people please God? What easy law did
God give Adam and Eve in the garden? What did
they have to do to please God? They could eat the
fruit of all the trees except one. That surely was
an easy law. Adam and Eve could have pleased
God if they just kept that law.

Oral Completion Test

1. When God commanded the good angels, they
. . . .

2. By obeying, the good angels . . . God.

3. Adam and Eve would have pleased God by
not eating the . . . .

Application   The angels pleased God by obeying Him. Adam
and Eve pleased God as long as they did not eat
of the forbidden fruit. If we wish to show God that
we love Him, we must do what He tells us. How
wicked it would be, if we did not want to be obedient to God after He has been so kind to us and
has given us so many good things! PROMISE THIS:
we will never do what God forbids; we will always
do what He wants; we will gladly do everything
He asks because we love Him. Then God will love
us and be pleased with us.

By and by I shall tell you everything that God

wants you to do and what He does not want you to do — what He commands and what He forbids. But you love God right now and you want to please Him right now, don't you? So make this promise with me: WHATEVER YOU TELL US THAT GOD COMMANDS, WE WILL DO. WHATEVER YOU SAY GOD FORBIDS, WE WILL NOT DO. WE WILL BE OBEDIENT TO GOD. That was a fine promise you made to God. If you keep that promise, you will be really loving God, you will be pleasing to Him, and He will love you.

Children, I know a special reason why you ought to try to please God now. You are going to receive your First Holy Communion in a short while. Then, dear Jesus, the Son of God, is coming into your heart. How good you ought to be! How hard you ought to try to please God!

Here is a little story that will show you how to try.[1] Many years ago there lived in a country far from here a father and mother and three little children, Madeleine, Julie, and their little brother, Louis. When Julie was born Madeleine was seven years old, and thought herself a big girl. While Julie was quite tiny her mother used to show her pictures of Jesus and taught her little prayers to say.

---

[1] "Blessed Julie" in *True Stories for First Communicants*, by a Sister of Notre Dame (London: Sands and Co.; St. Louis: B. Herder Book Company, 1919).

Later on Julie went to school. There the little boys and girls learned the Catechism and all about Almighty God. You should have seen Julie during those lessons. She did not play and fidget and look about, but with her eyes fixed on the teacher she seemed to drink in every word that he said.

Soon the priest noticed what a good little girl Julie was and how much she loved the good God. So he tried to help her to become even more holy. He taught her how to talk to Jesus in the tabernacle, and how to give up little things to show her love for God. He taught her, too, how to keep from getting angry when her little brother Louis teased her.

When the good priest saw how hard Julie tried to correct her faults and how well she prayed, he said he would let her make her First Holy Communion. But because she was so young, he said she must keep it a secret. How happy Julie was and how she longed for the day to come. At last the happy morning came.

Very, very early, before anyone was awake, little Julie got up. She hurried out of the house and down the street to the church. The good priest was waiting at the door for her, and together they went in. How empty the big church looked, but it did not feel empty to Julie, for Jesus was there. With folded hands she said the prayers for Holy Communion that the priest had taught her. Very piously Julie knelt on a little low chair and received her First Holy Communion.

All her life long Julie had a special love for Jesus in the tabernacle. When she grew up she taught others, too, to know and love our Lord in His little home on the altar. Jesus filled her heart full of love and joy in Him, so that she always kept singing in her heart: "Oh, how good is the good God."

The Our Father

"And lead us not into temptation . . . Amen."   *Prayer*

"Dear Angel Ever at My Side."[2]   *Song*

For Unit Two we would suggest a sand-table project of creation. Some valuable ideas for this are contained in *Practical Aids for Catholic Teachers*, pp. 227–230.[3] Suspend angels above the physical creation.   *Culminating Activity*

The principle of our absolute dependence upon the Creator and our consequent reaction of love toward Him is fundamental to all practical instruction. All subsequent lessons must be focused back to this point.   *Remarks*

---

[2] *Diocesan Hymnal I*, by Most Rev. Joseph Schrembs, D.D. (New York: J. Fischer & Bros.).

[3] *Practical Aids for Catholic Teachers*, by Sister M. Aurelia, O.S.F. and Rev. Felix M. Kirsch (New York: Benziger Bros., 1928).

UNIT THREE

Content

1. God is Everywhere and Knows All Things.
2. God Punishes Disobedience.
3. All the Children of Adam and Eve have their Sin and Punishment. God Promises the Redeemer.

Objectives

1. To understand and appreciate that God is everywhere and knows all things.
2. To develop an attitude of respect toward God and His decrees.
3. To appreciate more and more the Eucharistic Presence.
4. To learn how to make the accusation when receiving the Sacrament of Penance.
5. To learn how to make an Act of Contrition.

Part One

GOD IS EVERYWHERE AND KNOWS ALL THINGS

Picture   *Devices*

Eve Tempted by the Devil

Chalk Talks

Part I, p. 16.[1]

Introduction

You remember, children, what I told you last
time. Because God loved the angels so much and
made them so happy, what should they have done?   *Procedure*
And how could they please God? But not all the
angels were willing to remain obedient to God.
Some of them would not do what God wanted them
to do. What did God do with them after they became bad angels?

The good God, Who was so kind to the angels,
loved Adam and Eve, too. In return they should
have also loved God. How should they have shown
that they loved Him? What command did God give

---

[1]*Chalk Talks*, by Jerome F. O'Connor, S.J., and William
Hayden, S.J. (St. Louis: Queen's Work Press, 1928).

to them in the garden? What did He allow them
to do? What did He forbid them to do? As long as
Adam and Eve were obedient to God's command,
they showed that they loved Him. God also loved
them. For God loves those only who obey Him. He
does not love those who are disobedient. Now listen
to the story of what Adam and Eve did one day.

Presentation

One of those bad angels, who would not obey
God and who was cast into hell where he is very,
very unhappy, did not want Adam and Eve to remain obedient to God. He wanted them to do what
God had forbidden. So he hid himself in a snake
in the garden and said to Eve: "Why don't you eat
of the sweet fruits of this garden?" Eve answered:
"We do eat of these sweet fruits; but God told us
not to eat the fruit of one tree in the middle of the
garden. If we eat of it, we will have to die." The
bad angel said: "Oh, you will not die. If you eat of
it, then you will also know what is good or bad;
you will not have to keep any commandment of
God any more, and you may do as you please."
How sad! Eve listened to the words of the bad
angel. She kept looking at the forbidden fruit. It
seemed so nice and she thought it surely must
taste good. Slowly she raised her hand, took one

from the tree, bit into it, and gave it to Adam. He also ate of it.

Too bad! Too bad! for poor, disobedient Adam and Eve. God had loved them so much. They used to love God, too. He had done so many things to make them happy. They should have done the same for Him. How could they have pleased God? But what did they do instead? Now it is all changed. They are not good people any more. They are bad now. Before they had been so happy with God. But now they are afraid of Him. They hide themselves under the bushes and begin to tremble when they think of God. But God calls out: "Adam, where are you?" And poor Adam answers: "I heard Your voice, O God, but I am afraid of You." Then God says: "Adam, you are afraid because you ate of the fruit I told you not to:"

Recapitulation

See, children, what a sad story this is. It tells us of the first sin of Adam and Eve. Who did not want Adam and Eve to obey the good God? In what did he hide? What did he say to Eve? What did Eve answer? What did the bad angel promise Eve if she ate of the forbidden fruit? What did Eve do? How sad! God had loved Adam and Eve. He had been so kind to them. But they disobeyed Him anyway. Before their sin they had been happy with God. But how did they feel after their sin? Where did they hide? What did God say? What did Adam tell Him? What did God say when Adam told Him he was afraid?

Doctrinal. God is Everywhere — He Knows All Things

When Adam sinned, God said to him: "You are *Application* afraid because you ate of the fruit I told you not to." Children, what does that tell us about God? Who saw Adam and Eve when they did wrong? Yes, God was there when Adam and Eve sinned. They did not see Him, but still He knew everything they said or did or even thought about. God is not only in heaven. He was there in the garden with Adam and Eve. He is with us too. He is near us at home, in church, in school, on the street, out in the field, or in the woods. God is everywhere. But we cannot see Him, because He has no body.

Now pay attention! In my body there is a soul. You see my body, but you cannot see my soul. There is a soul in your body too. I see your body. Do I see your soul? It is like that with God. He is everywhere, but we cannot see Him. God knows all things, too, because He is everywhere.

God was there when Adam and Eve did wrong. He knew what they did. Could He still love them

after they were bad? Adam and Eve could not be
happy any more. After their sin they became very
sad. They were afraid, too. What did they do because they were afraid of God? Who saw them
anyway? What did God say to them? God told
Adam why he was afraid. Can you tell me why,
children?

Practical. God Sees My Sins — Telling Him My Sins

Now you have learned something more about
God, my dear children. You know that God is
everywhere and that He knows everything. How
glad you must feel when you think of this: God is
everywhere with me.

Who is here in school with us? Who hears what
I am telling you? You promised me before that
you would be obedient to God. Who heard you
make that promise? Who sees you when you are
naughty and disobedient in school? When Adam
and Eve were bad, God made them tell what they
did. You will have to tell God, too, when you are
disobedient in school. You will do that when you
go to confession. The priest will listen to your sins
in the place of God. This is how you would tell
God in confession that you were disobedient in
school: I WAS DISOBEDIENT TO MY TEACHER.

When you are at home with Daddy and Mother,

who is also there? Who sees everything you do
when you are home? Who hears and knows whatever you say to your parents, brothers and sisters,
and other people? Who knows if you disobey
Daddy or Mother or answer them back? Who
knows if you fight or quarrel with your brothers
and sisters? God wants you to tell Him those sins,
too, when you go to confession. The priest is God's
messenger. He will listen to your sins when you go
to confession. He will be kind and gentle to you
like Jesus is. If you were disobedient to your parents, this is how you would tell the priest: I WAS
DISOBEDIENT TO MY PARENTS. If you answered
them back, you would say: I ANSWERED MY PAR-
ENTS BACK WHEN THEY TOLD ME SOMETHING.
If you quarreled with your brothers and sisters,
you would say: I QUARRELED WITH MY BROTHERS
AND SISTERS. If you quarreled with your playmates, you would say: I QUARRELED WITH OTHER
CHILDREN.

Children, where does God look for you on Sun-
day morning? He sees when you are missing at
Sunday Mass. He calls after you when you stay
away through your own fault. You have to tell
Him that, too. You would say: I MISSED MASS ON
SUNDAY. He sees you also when you eat meat on
Friday. How would you tell God that you ate meat

on Friday? (*Have the children make their own form of accusation for this and the following sins. Make corrections where needed.*) God sees you when you steal something. He hears you when you tell lies. You must tell God in confession the sins you have done.

Children, when you remember: God is here! He saw it! He knows what bad thing I did! — then you are afraid of God just as Adam and Eve were. Oh! then you would like to hide from God as they did. But that did not help them; and it will not help you. God saw it anyway. He knows it. He cannot be pleased with you when you sin.

Think of this often, dear children: God is everywhere. He sees and knows all. Always behave well. Please God and be obedient to Him. Do you still remember who it was that tried to get the first people to sin? In what did he hide? The same way, there are bad people who try to make others bad; and there are bad children who want to make good children sin. You must never believe such bad children. If only Adam and Eve had not believed the bad angel! How happy they would have been!

Striking the Breast as a Sign of Sorrow

Children, now I shall tell you how to show God that you are sorry for your sins. Stand up! Put

Religious Practice

your left hand on your breast, as you do when making the sign of the cross. Now strike your breast with your right hand, just above the place where your left hand is. (*Do not let the children clench their right hand, but have them keep it open.*) That tells God that you are sorry. When you strike your breast like that, you might say: JESUS, I AM VERY SORRY FOR MY SINS. (*Practice with the class. Have individuals show how it is done.*)

Act of Contrition

Prayer

Perhaps, dear children, we have not always tried as we should to be good. Maybe we have sinned like Adam and Eve. If we have, we must tell God that we are very sorry. Let us learn a little prayer that tells the good God how sorry we are.

O Jesus, my God! I am very sorry
  that I have sinned against You.
You are so good, and my sins have hurt You.
  Help me, I will not sin any more.
      My Jesus, Mercy!

Remarks

In telling the Biblical story of Adam and Eve, we have drawn therefrom the qualities of God without entering into a detailed discussion of them. Our object was to make them appeal to the affections of the little ones and to lay the foundation for a correct understanding of these qualities at a later period in the child's life. Abstract expressions, like spirit, omnipresent, omniscient, were eschewed.

Part Two

GOD PUNISHES DISOBEDIENCE

Pictures

Devices

Adam and Eve Driven out of Paradise (Schumacher)

Jesus and the Child

Introduction

Children, it is easy to remember how much God loves us, because every day He gives us so many *Procedure* good things. Who will tell us some of the good things God gives us every day?

You also know where God is. Where is He? Where was God when Adam and Eve did what God told them not to do? Where is God when you are disobedient to Him? Who knows everything you do? How much does God know? Now tell me how long Adam and Eve were happy.

Yes, dear little ones, God wants us to be obedient to Him. If we are bad, He punishes us. He does something that hurts us. Here is how God punished Adam and Eve.

Presentation

God said to Eve: "I will let many sufferings come over you. You will have to suffer much with your children. You will have to be obedient to Adam, your husband."

Now hear how God punished Adam. God said to him: "You will have to work hard in the field; and even after your hard work, weeds and thorns will grow up. In the sweat of your brow you will have to earn your bread, until at last your body itself shall return to dust and earth. Both you and Eve shall die."

Then God sent them both out of the beautiful garden. (*Show the picture.*) How sad for Adam and Eve!

Adam and Eve did not die at once. They lived a long time. But at last they died. The good God punishes slowly, but surely. When the time came for them to die, the soul which gave their body life would have to leave that body. The soul, of course, would still be living. It cannot die. Now Adam and Eve had been very bad. Where do you think God could have sent their souls after they died? Do you still remember where God sent the angels who were bad? God can send people there too, if they are very bad. He could have sent the souls of Adam and Eve there. But soon we shall learn how the good God helped them again.

Recapitulation

God is so holy He cannot bear sin. He must punish those who disobey Him. How did He punish Adam and Eve? What did He say to Eve? What did He say to Adam? What did He say would happen to both of them at last?

Oral Completion Test

1. God punished Adam and Eve by sending them out of the . . . .

2. God punishes slowly, but . . . .

Doctrinal — God Punishes the Bad; He Rewards the Good

The good God sent Adam and Eve out of the *Application* beautiful garden. He told them they must die. See, children, how God punishes those who are disobedient to Him. But it serves them right. God punishes us, too, if we are disobedient to Him. It serves us right. God created us. He is our Lord and Master. We belong to Him. We must be obedient to Him. He loves us so much. We ought to love Him too. He makes us happy. We ought to please Him too. How do we please God? If we are disobedient to Him, we do not please Him and we do not love Him. It serves us right then, if God punishes us. Maybe He will not punish us right away. But He will punish us some day.

Children, you must be obedient to God, so that He does not punish you. God is everywhere with you. In all places He sees you and knows how you are acting. You must never do anything that God forbids. Every minute God makes you happy. He lets you live. He gives you many good things. So you must always, always please the good God by your obedience. A child that allows himself to be led to do bad will be afraid of God just as Adam and Eve were. Adam and Eve tried to hide themselves. It was no use, because God is everywhere. Neither can a bad child hide from God. As God punished Adam and Eve, so He will punish a bad child. Children, do you know where God could have sent the souls of Adam and Eve after the death of their bodies? So where can God send the soul of any person that is very bad?

We will all try to be good. We will please the good God by being obedient to Him. We will show that we really love Him by never doing anything that He forbids and always doing what He wants. Then He will love us. (*Show the picture of Jesus and the child nestling close to His Heart.*) Then we can be glad when we think: God is here with me, He is pleased with what I am doing. Then God will make us happier and happier, because He always pays richly for every good thing we do.

Liturgical — The Food that Gives Life

What did God say would happen to both Adam and Eve if they ate of the forbidden fruit? Yes, they did die too, as God had said, because they ate of the forbidden fruit. Eating of that forbidden fruit hurt Adam and Eve very much. It hurt their bodies and it hurt their souls.

But later when Jesus came into the world, He gave the people something to eat that would help them and make them good. Do you know what Jesus gave them to eat? It was a wonderful food. Yes, it was a food that came down from heaven. It was the very Body and Blood of Jesus. The dear, kind Jesus gave the people His own Body to eat, so that they would be good and holy. God had said to Adam and Eve: "If you eat of the forbidden fruit, you shall die." Jesus said to the people: "If you eat of this Bread, you shall live forever." Jesus meant this: those that eat His Body will live forever with Him in heaven. Who knows when we eat the Body of Jesus? Yes, when we receive Holy Communion. What a wonderful food Holy Communion is! How good Jesus was to give It to us. By and by we will learn more about this wonderful Food.

We would suggest that the little practices learned

Religious in the previous lessons be repeated: folding the
Practice hands at prayer, the sign of the cross, the genuflection, the greeting when passing a Catholic church
or a priest or a sister, the striking of the breast as
an act of sorrow. Have some of the children demonstrate to the class. The children of lesser talent
should be chosen this time. Some of these practices
might be correlated in reference to the reception of
Holy Communion: the striking of the breast at the
Domine non sum dignus; the folded hands, with
eyes cast down, gait slow and devout, in going to
and coming from the communion rail.

Part Three

ALL THE CHILDREN OF ADAM AND EVE INHERIT THEIR SIN AND PUNISHMENT — GOD PROM-ISES THE REDEEMER

Picture

Devices   Jesus the Savior

Introduction

Dear children! Adam and Eve committed sin.
Procedure They ate of the fruit which God had told them not
to eat. They were disobedient to the good God.

They wanted to do as they pleased. Now I must tell you something that is very, very sad.

Presentation

1. The disobedience of Adam and Eve hurt all people that came into the world after them. It hurts all of us who are now living. It will hurt every child that is born from now until the end of the world. We came into this world as bad children. If the good God had not helped us to be good again, so that He could be pleased with us, then nothing could have helped us.

Did you pay attention to what I just told you? What did I say? Who was hurt by the disobedience of the first people? Will those people who come into the world after us be hurt too? Later on you will learn of one person that was not hurt by this sin. But all the rest of the people were hurt by that one sin of disobedience.

2. You heard in the last lesson what God said to Eve. He told her she would have to suffer very much with her children, because she had been bad. Your mother, too, has to suffer like Eve. All mothers do. All mothers have many, many hard things to suffer with their children. You remember also what God told Adam he would have to suffer. Adam had to suffer just as God had said. He had to work

hard, plowing the earth and planting things. But even after all his hard work, weeds and thorns grew. Didn't you ever notice how hard your father has to work? How tired he is when he comes home at night! But even after all his hard work, things are not always right. God told Adam he would have to earn his bread in the sweat of his brow. Look at your parents! See how they have to sweat at their work! Adam and Eve were sent out of the beautiful garden because they were bad. We cannot live in this beautiful garden either. We suffer from the heat, from the cold; we have troubles and accidents. Who still remembers what God told Adam and Eve would happen to them in the end, if they ate of the forbidden fruit? What would become of their bodies? Yes, both of them died. What happens at last to all of us? Today an old person dies; tomorrow, a young person; some other day, a little baby. All people must die. There you see how the badness of the first two people hurts us all.

3. Adam and Eve's hearts, too, became bad after their sin. They felt like being disobedient. They felt like doing what God told them not to do. They liked to do just what they wanted and not what God wanted.

Children, some time ago you promised me that you would be obedient to God and try to please

Him. To do that, you must watch over yourself. Tell me honestly: don't you easily forget God? don't you like to play rather than study? don't you have to do something hard to study? when you should be thinking of God, doesn't your play very often come to mind instead? when your parents tell you to do something, don't you find it hard sometimes to do it quickly? I am sure you would have to answer "yes" to all these questions. You do not always feel like doing what God wants. It is easier to do just as you please. See, children, that is the badness in us. This badness comes to us from the sin of Adam and Eve. They were made bad by their sin. We, too, are made bad by their sin.

Children, we must work hard to fight against our badness. But we cannot do it alone, any more than Adam and Eve could. God must help us. You know, too, that as long as we are bad, God cannot love us. If God does not help us, our soul cannot go to Him in heaven when our body dies. How sad that our soul is bad when we come into this world! That is because of Adam and Eve's disobedience to God.

But the good, great God can help us. How much can God do, children? How does God feel toward us?

4. Yes, God has helped! To Adam and Eve, God

promised to send a person who would make the
bad people good again. This person would make
the good God forgive the sins of the people. He
would have the good God open the gates of heaven
again to good people. This person we call the Redeemer of the world, the Savior of men. (*Show the
picture of Jesus the Savior.*) O good Savior, how
glad we are that You came to help us! (*Repeat,
and have the class say it together.*)

Recapitulation

Now you have just heard many great things. Let
me see how many of them you can remember. Who
was hurt by the disobedience of Adam and Eve?
Who still has to feel the punishment that Adam
and Eve received? How is our soul because of the
sin of the first two people? We do not like to be
obedient to God. We would rather do as we please.
We easily forget God. We would rather do what we
want than what God wants. Do we find it easy to
be good? If God does not help us, where will our
soul go after our body dies? Whom did God promise to send to help us? What name do we give to
that Person Who came to help us? What little
prayer to the Savior do you know?

Application   You know, dear children, that it is not easy to be
good. You have to try, and try, and try. Do you

want to hear a little story that will tell you how to try?

Mary was a little girl, just as old as you are. She had a good daddy and a very dear mother. But her poor mother had been sick in bed ever since Mary had been a tiny tot. The neighbors all felt sorry for Mary's mother and almost every day some one of them would come to pay her a visit. Often they would bring in a cake or some fruit for their sick neighbor. Mary, too, was good to her mother. When she came home from school, the first place she went was to mother's bedside to ask how she was getting along and to see if she could go on any errands.

One afternoon when Mary came into the sick-room, she found her mother asleep. Mary's eyes wandered about the room. There on a table she spied a nice, big basket of oranges, apples, and bananas. Mary looked at it long. How she would like one of those apples! But she remembered that her mother had always taught her never to take anything from the house without asking. Just a few days ago, the Sister at school had told them the same thing. Poor Mary! She wanted an apple so much, but she knew that she should not take one without her mother's permission. The devil was whispering into her ear: "Oh, don't mind! Just take one anyway. See how good they are!" But her Guardian Angel whispered: "Don't do it!"

Mary listened to the devil. Taking a big, red-cheeked apple from the basket, she hurried into the kitchen. She was just about to take a bite. But her Guardian Angel whispered again: "Mary, what are you doing? Don't you know that God sees you? You should not have taken that apple without asking your mother. Hurry, take it back!"

Little Mary became afraid. Quickly she tiptoed back into her mother's room with the apple. Bravely she put it back into the basket. As she did so, her mother who had just awakened from her sleep heard her say: "Jesus, I'm putting it back. I'm sorry I took it."

See, children, how hard Mary had to try to be good. We, too, must try, and try, and try to do what is right and good. Let us ask God to help us. O GOOD AND GREAT GOD, HELP US TO DO ALWAYS WHAT IS RIGHT.

Prayer Repeat the Our Father and the Act of Contrition. Drill both in their entirety. Tell the children that the prayers they learn should be said not only in school and in church, but also at home. The prayers at home should be said especially in the morning and at night — morning prayers and night prayers.

For Unit Three we would suggest that the children begin a religion booklet. This might be continued throughout the remainder of the course. The main or dominating theme of all the pictures put into this booklet should be Holy Communion. Suggestions for this activity can be found in *Art Education Through Religion,* Books I and II.[1]   *Culminating Activity*

For this Unit, two or three pictures could be pasted by the children into their religion booklet. The subjects of these pictures might be: Jesus Friend of Children, A Child at the Feet of Jesus the Good Shepherd, A Child in the Arms of Jesus.

In this and the previous instruction, you will notice the exactness with which the punishment of Adam and Eve is described, and likewise the transmission of their sin to us, as shown in our corruption. The revealed teaching of the Church has been closely followed, though in childlike language. In the previous instruction the punishment consequent upon the sin of our first parents was described under three aspects: (*a*) the interior restlessness of Adam and Eve; (*b*) the positive penalties inflicted by God; (*c*) the status of the soul after the death of the body. Notice how logically the dogma of the necessity of the Redeemer follows from these lessons. The transmission of the first sin upon the whole human race was shown not merely in the continuation of its punishment in this life, but principally   *Remarks*

[1] *Art Education Through Religion,* Books I and II, by Mary Gertrude McMunigle (New York: Mentzer, Bush & Co., 1930).

in that inherent wickedness of our souls and in our inability to attain eternal happiness of ourselves. This presentation is in harmony with the teaching of the Council of Trent which says: "The sin of our first parents brought not only death and corporal punishment upon the whole race, but sin itself, which is the death of the soul. That sin is each one's own and can be removed neither by human means nor any other, except the merits of the One Mediator, our Lord Jesus Christ." (*Council of Trent, Section 5, decree on original sin.*) In explaining this doctrine to the children, we simply said: "we could not enter heaven on account of this sin in which we were born."

In these instructions we have avoided the expression "original sin." The idea of original sin, however, was presented to the child's emotional life. We said: "we are miserable because of the sin of our first parents; we are unable of ourselves to do good; positive corruption is inborn in our soul; only God can help us; He has helped us through the Savior." The idea of God's mercy has not been further emphasized for two reasons: (*a*) children in these tender years are guilty of only few actual sins; (*b*) they are incapable of assimilating the idea of what is required for sorrow, amendment, and conversion. To convey the notion that God forgives sin and reinstates man in His good pleasure without the fulfillment of these conditions, would give the false impression that God forgives without penance and conversion on our part.

UNIT FOUR

Content

1. The Savior's Coming is Announced.
2. The Savior is Born to Us.
3. Jesus is Born Every Day on our Altars; Holy Mass.

Objectives

1. To inflame our hearts with love for Jesus, our Savior.
2. To develop an attitude of reverence and obedience toward Him.
3. To see and know Jesus not merely as an historical Person, but as One living in our midst under the Eucharistic veil.
4. To know how to say the Hail Mary.

Part One

THE SAVIOR'S COMING IS
ANNOUNCED

Pictures

Mary the Maiden
The Annunciation (Schumacher)

Introduction

God let many long years pass before He sent the
promised Savior. Adam and Eve were very sorry *Procedure*
for their disobedience. They did penance as long
as they lived. Every day they hoped for the Savior
to come. So did the good people after them. They
hoped that the Savior would move God to forgive
their sins. Many times they cried out: "Oh! if God
would only send Him." At last God did send the
Savior. Listen, children, while I tell you how that
happened.

Presentation

In a country far away from here, where the Jews
used to live, there was a very pious girl, the Virgin
Mary. (*Show a picture of the Virgin Mary.*) She

was poor, but holy. She was engaged to be married to a poor carpenter, whose name was Joseph. He was pious and good too.

One day, God sent one of his great prince-angels, Gabriel, down to Mary. (*Show the picture of the angel.*) God sent this angel to Mary to tell her that she would be the mother of the Savior. That day the holy Virgin was all alone in her little room in the little town of Nazareth. All of a sudden the Angel Gabriel stood before her.

"Hail! Mary," said the angel, "full of grace; the Lord is with thee; blessed art thou among women." Listen, children, and I shall tell you the meaning of the angel's words. "I greet you, holy Virgin Mary. You are a special friend of God. God loves you very much. He helps you more than He helps anyone else. He has chosen you out of all women to receive a special favor."

Holy Mary was afraid when she saw the angel and heard him say this. Then the Angel Gabriel spoke again.

"Do not be afraid. You are a special friend of God. You shall receive a Son. Call Him Jesus. Jesus means Savior The Holy Ghost shall come over you; and this Son, Whom you will receive, shall be the Son of God."

Mary was afraid because such a great thing was going to happen to her. But she said to the angel:

"I am the servant of God. Let it be done as you have said."

Then the angel went away, back to heaven.

Recapitulation

Tell me, children, what I have just said. What was the Virgin's name to whom the Angel Gabriel was sent by God? What kind of person was this Virgin? Why did God love her so much? To whom was she engaged to be married? Where did she live? When the angel was sent to Mary, how did he greet her? When Mary became afraid, what did the angel tell her? What name was she to give her Son? What does Jesus mean? And Who, did the angel say, would come over Mary? Whose Son was this Jesus? See, children, you have just told me the three Persons of God: the Father, the Son, and the Holy Ghost — God the Father, God the Son, and God the Holy Ghost. What little prayer do you know in which these three holy names are used? Yes, the sign of the cross. Now one more question, children. What did the Virgin Mary say to the angel?

1. You told me before, dear children, that the Virgin Mary was a holy person. God loves holy *Application* people, people who are pious. If pious people are poor, God loves them anyway. If people are rich but not pious, God does not love them. God does

not look to see if we are rich or poor before He loves us. How must we be if we want Him to love us? Yes, children, we must try our very best to be holy and pious. Then God will love us. He will love us each day more and more. Now tell me some things a pious child will do.

2. What did holy Mary say when the angel told her that she was to be the mother of the Savior? That showed that the Virgin Mary was obedient. She wanted to do what God told her. She said: "I am the servant of God." A servant must do everything right away when the Master tells her. God is my Master. He is your Master too. He is everyone's Master. We are all servants of God. So what must we do when God commands? How good it was that the Virgin Mary was obedient to God. Was Eve obedient to God? No, and because Eve disobeyed God, we all became unhappy and bad. But Mary obeyed, and the Savior came into the world to make us happy and good again.

The Small Sign of the Cross

Children, you already know one way of making
Religious the sign of the cross. Stand up and we shall make
Practice it together. The sign of the cross we have just made is called the large sign of the cross. I am going to show you another way of making the sign of the

cross. It is called the small sign of the cross. This is how you make the small sign of the cross.

Open your right hand, the fingers straight out and together, the thumb apart. Put your left hand on your breast, as you do for the large sign of the cross. Now with the thumb of your right hand trace a small cross on your forehead, another on your lips, and a third one just near your heart. (*Demonstrate to the children, have them do it together with you, and then have individuals do it alone before the class.*)

When you make the small sign of the cross, you may say these words. As you trace the cross on your forehead, say: "Jesus, be in my mind." On the lips: "Jesus, be on my lips." Near the heart: "Jesus, be in my heart."

You may make the small sign of the cross two times during Mass — at the First Gospel and at the Last Gospel, when the priest walks over to the left side of the altar, and when the people in church all stand up.

Hail Mary

(Teach the first half of the prayer with Part One. As a means of linking the first portion of the Hail Mary with the Annunciation in the child's mind, the story of the Annunciation might be *Prayer* dramatized. The exact words of the Hail Mary, up to and including the words "blessed is the fruit of thy womb, Jesus," could be used, despite the slight historical inaccuracy.)

Our Classroom Crib

Activity As soon as Unit Four is begun, it would be well to have the children start their work on the classroom crib. This could be kept in the room throughout the year or at least during the instructions up to Holy Week, since the crib is the most appropriate center for the little ones' devotion. In the making of the crib, as much work and material as possible should be furnished by the children themselves. Suggestions for modeling statues for the crib can be found in *Art Education Through Religion*, Book II.[1]

Remarks Notice how the simple telling of the story of the Annunciation is used as a preparation for imparting the teachings of the Church. The Blessed Trinity and the reinstatement of mankind through Christ is touched upon in passing. The obedience of Mary is contrasted with the disobedience of Eve — a thought borrowed from the Fathers, principally St. Augustine. Observe also how the ideas of holy love and of obedience that is born of love are developed.

---

[1] *Art Education Through Religion*, Book II, by Mary Gertrude McMunigle (New York: Mentzer, Bush & Co., 1930).

Part Two

THE ŚAVIOR IS BORN TO US

Object

The Classroom Crib   *Devices*

Pictures

The Nativity (Schumacher)
Mary and the Infant

Introduction

In our last lesson, children, we heard some good
news from heaven. We heard the Angel Gabriel tell *Procedure*
Holy Mary that Jesus, the Savior, was soon coming. How good it was of Holy Mary to say that
she would be the mother of Jesus! Today, I shall
tell you the story of how Infant Jesus was born.

Presentation

1. Some months after the angel had come to
Mary, there was another visitor at the little home
of Joseph and Mary in Nazareth. This time it was
not a beautiful angel, but a rough man with a
rough voice, who told Mary and Joseph that they
had to go to the city of Bethlehem. This rough man

was sent by the king, so Mary and Joseph obeyed at once.

It was night when they came to Bethlehem. You can imagine that they were tired and sleepy after their long trip. Joseph tried to find a place where they could stay over the night, but wherever he asked he was told that there was no room. At last he found a place, an old barn where the people used to keep their animals. Poor Mary and Joseph! And Baby Jesus was coming soon.

All was quiet now. Suddenly a bright, golden light filled the barn and Baby Jesus came. Holy Mother Mary wrapped her Babe in the poor little clothes she had brought along for Him. Then she laid Him in the only little bed she could find in the barn, a crib or manger from which the animals ate their food. (*Show the picture of the Nativity.*) Dear children, look at the Infant Jesus! See how poor He was when He came into this world to be our Savior!

2. In a field near by, shepherds were watching their sheep through the night. Suddenly a bright light shone around them. An angel, shining like the sun, stood before them. The shepherds were afraid. They began to tremble. Then the angel spoke: "Fear not! I have good news for you; good news for all men. The Savior has been born in Bethlehem. He

will save all men. You can find Him easily. He is in a stable, lying in the manger, wrapped in baby's clothes. He is the Savior of all men." Then the shepherds saw many, many angels. The angels were singing and praising God. This is the song they sang. "Glory to God in the highest; and on earth, peace to men of good will!"

In a moment the angels were gone. The bright light was gone, too. The shepherds hurried over to Bethlehem and found the Infant Jesus in the stable, wrapped up in little clothes, and lying in a manger. They were very happy. They adored Jesus and gave Him their love. When they got back home, they told their friends what they had seen and heard.

Recapitulation

1. Children, we have just heard how Jesus came into the world as a Babe. He was the Son of God, as the angel had told His Mother; and He came to save all men. What is the name of the city to which Mary and Joseph went? Where did they have to stay for the night? Why did they have to stay in a stable or barn? What happened that night? What did Holy Mother Mary do with her Child? Where did she put Him?

2. What happened in a field near by? To whom did

the angel tell the news that Jesus was born? What did all the angels do? Yes, God be praised that the Savior has come. Those who are good and who believe in the Savior, the Son of God, are always happy.

Application 1. Children, we learned that the Infant Jesus came into this world as a poor Babe. Where did His Blessed Mother have to lay Him? Just think! Jesus, the Son of God, was poor. How should we feel if we are poor? Yes, we should think: "I will be glad to be poor, because Jesus was poor. God loved the poor Infant Jesus; He will love me, too."

2. Dear children! Each Christmas day we think of the birthday of Jesus. He was born in the middle of the night. For that reason many grown-up people go to church at midnight on Christmas. They are happy about the birth of Jesus. They thank Him for it.

You have already seen the crib in church at Christmas time. We have just finished our classroom crib, too. There you see Joseph and Mary in the stable, and the wee little Child Jesus lying in the manger. Some of the shepherds kneel in front of the Child. Others are hurrying to Him with their presents. Above the stable roof, you see an angel praising God. This angel holds in his hands a ribbon on which is written: Glory to God in the highest. The crib, dear children, is a picture of the story of how Jesus was born.

When you look at the crib during Christmas time, be glad that Jesus was born. Love Him, because He loved you so much in coming as a poor Babe into this world. Promise Him you will do whatever I tell you He wants you to do, because you love Him. Then you will be real pious, holy children. You will love God, and God will love you.

Simple little Christmas hymns should be sung by the children as they gather around the crib. The little ones should be told that these hymns are prayers which they sing to the Infant Jesus.

Religious Practice

During the course of this lesson, individuals of the class could be told to do certain things around the crib. Before the birth of the Infant Jesus, some could help to tidy up the stable, smooth out the straw, and other little chores. They should be constantly reminded that they are doing these things for the coming of Jesus. After His birth, the others could approach the crib to perform little devotions for the Child Jesus. In giving these little commands to the children, it would be a good thing to make use of the "Reading Slips," as suggested in the Montessori method. These reading slips would have a simple command, written by the teacher, which the child on reading would execute himself. For

Activity

example, one slip might read: Go to the crib and
make the sign of the cross for Baby Jesus.

Hail Mary

Prayer   (Teach the second half of the Hail Mary. Have
the children look at the crib. Let them point out
holy Mary and the Infant Jesus. Then show them
a large picture of Holy Mary with the Infant Jesus
in her arms.)

Who is that? Yes, holy Mary. And who is that?
Jesus, her little Son. Holy Mary is the Mother of
Jesus. And Jesus is God. "Holy Mary, Mother of
God." See! She is looking at Jesus and talking to
Him. What do you think she is talking about? Does
holy Mary love us? Maybe she is talking to Jesus
about us. Maybe she is asking Him something for
us. Holy Mary loves us very much, and she asks her
Son Jesus many times for us. "Holy Mary, Mother
of God, pray for us sinners, now and at the hour of
our death. Amen."

Song   ### Hail Mary[1]

Remarks   Note how the common practices of the Church and
her liturgy are woven into the instruction at the oppor-
tune time. These two, doctrine and liturgy, are com-

---

[1]*Diocesan Hymnal I,* by Most Reverend Joseph Schrembs,
D.D. (New York: J. Fischer & Bros., 1928).

bined, so that these figures and practices of the Church do not become merely empty, meaningless things.

Part Three

JESUS IS BORN EVERY DAY ON OUR ALTARS — HOLY MASS

This instruction is best given in the church itself. Candles may be lighted on the altar and if the *Devices* catechist is a priest he may vest in surplice to dispose himself and the children to the deepest reverence.

The monstrance or a large picture of it will be needed to show to the children.

Introduction

Dear children! God loved us so much that He sent His only Son down to this earth to be born *Procedure* as a little Babe. Jesus became our Baby Brother. Oh! how Jesus loved us! He came as a poor little Babe in a poor little stable. Today, I am going to tell you something that will show how much Jesus still loves us.

Presentation

1. See the beautiful little house in the middle of the altar! It is called the tabernacle. It has a gold-

en door. Sometimes the priest opens the door. He
looks into the little house, and then quickly kneels
down. Ah! there must be Someone very holy in
there, because the priest kneels down. Yes, children,
the dear Child Jesus is in there. The priest kneels
down before the Child Jesus. Jesus is the Son of
God, you know. Now you are looking up at the
little house, too. You are thinking to yourself: oh!
if I could only see the little Child Jesus.

(*Show the monstrance or a large picture of it to
the children.*) Did you ever see this before when
you were in church? It is made of gold. People call
it the monstrance. I will tell you what it is used
for. Sometimes the priest goes to the altar, opens
the little door, and kneels down. He takes Jesus out
of the little house and puts Him in the center of the
golden monstrance. Jesus has made Himself very,
very small, even much smaller than a little child.
Little Jesus was also in the crib. Holy Mary
wrapped Him in white clothes. You could only see
His little head and His little arms. But in the monstrance He is all covered up.

Now listen! With the snow-white Child Jesus in
the monstrance, the priest turns about and makes
the sign of the cross over the people. Jesus beneath
the white veil also lifts His hand and blesses the
people. He loves best to bless little children. Good

children are happy when the Child Jesus blesses them. They look up to Jesus. They are so glad to see Him. While they are looking at Jesus, they say: "My Lord and my God!" (*Practice these words with the children.*) Then they make the sign of the cross on themselves or strike their breast.

2. You want to ask me a question now, don't you? How does the Child Jesus come on the altar? Well, the Child Jesus lives in that little house on the altar. The priest puts Him in there. The priest opens the door to take Him out. The priest is the only one who can do this. The priest is the one who calls Jesus down from heaven to the altar. Jesus told the priest to do this. Every morning the priest calls Jesus, and Jesus comes down quickly from heaven to the altar. In heaven Jesus is very big and great; but when He comes on the altar, He makes Himself very, very small.

3. Do you know, children, why Jesus makes Himself so small? He does that, because He wants to come into your little heart. He doesn't want to stay in that little house on the altar, all alone. He wants to come to you. He wants the priest to open the little golden door, to take Him out, and to give Him to you. You have seen people go up to the front of the church to the railing. They go up there to get Jesus. The priest will give Jesus to them.

Some day you will go up to the altar, and then the priest will give you the Child Jesus. You will take Jesus right into your heart. How happy you will be then! You must be good now so that Jesus will be glad to come into your heart.

Recapitulation

1. Children, Who lives in the little golden house on the altar? When the priest opens the door, what does he do right away? Why does he kneel down? I told you that the priest sometimes puts the Child Jesus in the monstrance. When he turns around with the monstrance, what does he do over the people? Who really blesses the people? Jesus makes Himself very small. When you see the Child Jesus in the monstrance, all covered up and so very, very small, of what do you think? What does a good child say when it looks up at Jesus? What does a good child do?

2. Who puts Jesus into the tabernacle? Who takes Him out? Can anyone else do that? Who calls Jesus down to the altar? Who alone can do that? From where does Jesus come? How often does the priest call Jesus down to the altar?

3. Can you tell me why Jesus makes Himself so small? Into whose heart does He want to come?

Why do people go up to the railing in the front of the church? Some day you will go there, too, to get Jesus. The day on which you receive Jesus for the first time will be the happiest day of your life. What must you do if you want Jesus to come? Say with me: JESUS, JESUS, COME TO ME!

How the Little Ones Should Assist at Mass

1. *With outward respect.* Very much depends upon the way the children have been taught to reverence the house of God. Before they understand what a tremendous mystery takes place at the altar, they must have that reverential feeling that the place in which the priest prays is a holy place. If *reverence has been* instilled in the children's hearts, one will not have to remind them often nor threaten nor punish them. Once deeply planted, reverence in the house of God will become an enduring habit of their lives. *Application*

A certain amount of external control is absolutely necessary. Children are naturally restless. They must know that the eye of the teacher or priest is upon them during divine services. If they forget themselves, they must be brought to order by a look of disapproval. The teacher or priest must not neglect to go through the aisles *occasionally* to lift a fallen hand, to turn a head in the right direction, to help an unknowing hand form the sign of the cross, to make a careless child kneel straight.

The catechist should let the children know that he is fully aware of the way they behave in church. He should show joy when the children have been well behaved; sorrow, when they have been guilty of grave misconduct. He must praise the good; the bad, he must scold. The motive presented both in praise and in blame should be love and respect for Jesus.

2. *With attention.* Although the important thing in the primary grades is to get the children to behave well in church, the matter of the attentive hearing of Mass should not be neglected. In fact, outward decorum without attention cannot last for any length of time. The prerequisite for attention is interest. To be interested, these little children must be able to see the altar and what goes on there. The children's interest should first center around those things which they can most readily observe; namely, the altar and those persons who take an active part in the services. One should not imagine that this interest will come or continue of itself. In the beginning, of course, when the altar and all that takes place there is new to

the children, they will look on with interest. Soon, however, the stimulus of novelty will disappear; and with it, attention. Playing and trifling will then begin. Accordingly, the catechist must ever be on the alert to direct anew the children's attention and interest to the altar and whatever transpires there.

The catechist will give his children easy tasks in *observation*. For example, he will have them count the steps that lead up to the altar and tell the results in the next class; or the candles on the altar, to tell how many were lighted; or he will have them give an account of the color of the vestments used at Mass.

He may also let them describe what the priest did at the altar. The children, as a rule, will put plenty of life into this. One child has noticed this, another has observed something else. The child's natural impulse to imitate should also be utilized. One or other child, especially the boys, should imitate something that they have noticed the priest doing at the altar. For example, let one of the boys show how the priest turned around at the altar and what he did then; or how the priest sprinkled the people with holy water. These are only small details; but thus the child accustoms itself to observe the altar and the actions that go on there.

Religion Booklet

Pictures of the altar with its crucifix and candles may be cut out and pasted in the religion booklet; also pictures of the chalice, tabernacle, and other familiar objects connected with the altar.[1]

The Home Altar

Children can be shown how to make, arrange, and decorate an altar in their own homes. Good children love to do this. It will be noticed how such children will look up to the altar in church with so much more interest. The child's soul, so to speak, will grow with the altar. This is the necessary foundation for later devotion at Mass.

The instruction on the Holy Mass for the small children is not systematically built up. It is given piecemeal as occasion offers. Thus the story of the Offering of Jesus in the Temple gives occasion to speak of the Offering of Jesus at the Consecration; the story of the Last Supper permits one to speak of Transubstantiation. The method for small children is *psychological* rather than logical in development. This present instruction[2] serves merely to bring together the building stones for future, systematic understanding of the Holy Mass. It

---

[1] Cf. *Art Education Through Religion,* Book II, p. 35.

[2] Adapted from the instruction of Rev. J. Minnichthaler, incorporated in the Appendix of Father Gatterer's *Elementarkatechesen,* pp. 228–236.

lays deep the elements of devotion at Mass; namely, faith in the sacramental Jesus and love toward Him.

It is better for the children of the first grade *not to use a prayer book*. As a general rule, very young children are tempted by the pictures to a meaningless paging of their prayer book. Thereby, they are kept from looking at the altar, and from observing the sacred actions that take place there.

UNIT FIVE

Content

1. Childhood Friends of Jesus: The Wise Men.
2. Childhood Friends of Jesus: Simeon and Anna.
3. Jesus at Twelve.

Objectives

1. To appreciate God's fatherly love in giving us Jesus.
2. To recognize that we ought to be obedient to God for reasons of gratitude, love, and childlike humility rather than moral necessity.
3. To know the Acts of Faith, Hope, and Love.

Part One

CHILDHOOD FRIENDS OF JESUS:
THE WISE MEN

Pictures

The Journey of the Magi
The Adoration of the Magi (Schumacher)

Devices

Introduction

The shepherds were not the only ones who were *Procedure*
told of the coming of Jesus, the Savior. There were
some other pious men who found out that Jesus was
born. Listen carefully while I tell you about them.

Presentation

In a far-away country, there lived some pious
men who were very rich and great. One night they
saw a star in the heavens that they had never seen
before. God put into their minds that this star
meant the Savior was born. They had heard of the
Savior long before, because God had promised to
send Him. At once these pious men said they would
look for the Savior. They wanted to honor Him.
They wanted to show Him how glad they were that
He was born. So they got some of their best things

to give Him as presents. They took gold, frankincense, and myrrh.

Gold is the best kind of money. Frankincense is
a gum that comes from a tree. It is dropped on hot
coals and makes a smoke that smells like perfume.
Did you ever notice in church how the priest puts
incense on hot coals and how the smoke rises before the altar? Myrrh is also gumlike. It is used
to keep the body of a dead person from turning so
soon to dust and ashes. It is also used as medicine
for sick people.

These pious men then started out on their journey. There were three men. We call them the Three
Wise Men. They watched the star and kept following it. (*Show the picture.*)

At last they came to Jerusalem, the greatest city
in the land of the Jews. The king lived there. The
Wise Men asked him where the newborn Savior
was. But the newborn Savior was not in Jerusalem.
The people did not know about Him there. The
priests told the Wise Men that many, many years
before God had said through a pious man that the
Savior would be born in Bethlehem. Then they
showed these pious travelers the way to Bethlehem.

When the travelers left the city of Jerusalem and
came on to the road to Bethlehem, the star was
shining again in the heavens. It was straight above

the road. The holy travelers were happy again and
followed the star. When they came near Bethlehem,
the star stood still above a stable. They went in
and found holy Joseph, holy Mother Mary, and
the little Child Jesus. (*Show picture.*) The three
Wise Men were very happy. They believed that the
Child, to Whom God brought them, was the Redeemer of the world. They knelt down to pray and
then gave Jesus their gold, frankincense, and
myrrh. After a while they went back to their own
country again. On the way home they felt very,
very happy.

Recapitulation

Now children, I'll see how much you can remember of this story. The shepherds of Bethlehem, you
know, were the first to learn that the Savior was
born. Who told them? Who else found out about
Jesus? What did the Wise Men see in the heavens?
What did God tell them was the meaning of this
strange star? What did they do right away? To
Whom did they want to go? They were good, pious
men who loved God. As soon as God put some good
thought into their minds, they obeyed Him at once.
God told them the star meant the Savior was born.
What did they do right away? How did they feel
in their hearts? What did they want to do to show

God how glad and thankful they were to Him? What did they take with them?

Oral Completion Test

1. When God told the Wise Men what the star meant, at once they . . . .

2. When God tells us something, like the Wise Men we should . . . .

Practical

See! the presents of the Wise Men were just the
Application right things for the Redeemer of the world. Gold — because Jesus is the highest Lord of all. Frankincense, which we burn in church before the altar of God — because Jesus is the Son of God. Myrrh — because Jesus died for us.

Children, you often hear me telling you what God wants you to do. He wants you to learn your lessons well, to be obedient, to pray nicely. You yourselves think, too, of what God wants you to do. When that comes to your mind, you should do it, just as the pious men did. They were glad when they saw the star. You should be glad when you learn what God wants you to do. They were happy to follow the star. You should be happy to do whatever God wants of you. Then you will be good children. God will be pleased with you. Promise me now and promise God that you will always do what He wants.

This story of the pious men is shown for you in church on the Feast of the Three Kings. There you see the three men with their servants. They are carrying their presents of gold, frankincense, and myrrh to the Child Jesus. When you see that in church, of what story should you think? What should you then promise God? God doesn't want you to bring gold, frankincense, and myrrh to Him. You haven't these things. But God wants you to give Him obedience. You can be obedient like these pious men. You can pray to Jesus, too, just as these Wise Men did. Then God will be pleased with you, as He was pleased with them and their gifts.

Liturgical

The Tabernacle Light. God used a wonderful bright star to show the Wise Men where the Child Jesus was. When the star stood still over the stable, these pious men knew that the Savior was there. The star seemed to say: "Here we are at last! This is the home of Jesus. Give Him your presents and pray to Him."

Children, did you ever see anything in church that reminds you of the star which led the Wise Men to Jesus? It is near the tabernacle. It is a bright little light that burns all day and all night to tell us that Jesus is there. The tabernacle light seems to say: "Come, little child, for Jesus lives here. Bring Him your presents and pray to Him."

Good children are glad to visit Jesus. Jesus likes to have them come to Him. When St. Thérèse was still a little child she knew how anxious Jesus was to have her visit Him in the church. She often used to beg her nurse to take her to church when they went for their afternoon walk. Later on her father took her for a walk each day and they always went into the church for a visit to Jesus. Little Thérèse did not know any long, beautiful prayers at that time. But she said her little, childlike prayers with all her heart. Jesus loved Thérèse for coming to visit Him. He was pleased, too, with her simple, little prayers.

Act of Faith

Prayer   Today I shall teach you a little prayer that Jesus likes to hear you say.

> O my God! I believe every word
>   You have said,
> Because You are God and what You say
>   is always true.

Lovely Infant, Dearest Savior[1]   *Hymn*

Paper Cutting[2]   *Activity*

1. The Christmas Star
2. Camel

This and the following instruction have not been ar-
ranged in their historical sequence. We have placed the   *Remarks*
story of the Three Kings first, because the characters
are more familiar to the children.

Part Two

CHILDHOOD FRIENDS OF JESUS: SIMEON AND ANNA

Pictures

The Presentation (Schumacher)
A Child's Communion   *Devices*

Introduction

Whom did God tell to follow a strange star? See!
we have already heard of several people who were   *Procedure*

---

[1]*Diocesan Hymnal II* (p. 5), by Most Reverend Joseph
Schrembs, D.D.

[2]*Art Education Through Religion*, Books I and IV, by
Mary Gertrude McMunigle.

told of the birth of the Savior. Who were they? Yes, Mary and Joseph; the shepherds; and the three Wise Men. All of these people were very happy when they saw the Savior. Today I am going to tell you of two other persons who were made very, very happy by the little Infant Jesus.

Presentation

When Jesus was forty days old, St. Joseph and holy Mother Mary took Him to church in the city of Jerusalem. They thanked the good God for giving them the Child Jesus and offered a gift of two doves. There were two other people in the church that day who knew from God that Jesus was the Savior. These were two very pious and holy people. They lived in Jerusalem and both were very old. The man's name was Simeon; the woman's name was Anna.

Simeon had often prayed that God would soon let the Savior come into the world. One day while he was praying for this, God the Holy Ghost put into his mind that he would not die before the Savior had come. That day when holy Mary and St. Joseph carried the Child Jesus to the church, Simeon kept thinking and thinking that he ought to go to church. It was God whispering to him, so Simeon obeyed. The pious old man got ready and

went to church. There he saw the Child Jesus in
the arms of His holy Mother. Then God whispered
to him that this Child was the Redeemer of the
world. With a happy heart, Simeon took the Child
from holy Mary, held Him in his own arms, and
said: "O God! now let me die because I have seen
with my own eyes the promised Savior." (*Show
picture.*)

Then holy Anna came by. She also believed that
this Child was the Savior. She praised God and
quickly went out to tell other good people what
she had seen in the church. (*Point out on the
picture.*)

Recapitulation

See, children, to how many good people God told
the news that the Savior of the world was born.
Who found out in church that the Child Jesus was
the Redeemer? What did pious Simeon often do?
When he prayed like that, what did God the Holy
Ghost put into his mind? Do you know Who
whispered to him to go to church that day when
holy Mary took the child there? Simeon went to
church then. Whom did he find there? Who told
him that this Child was the Savior? Who else found
out in church that this Child was the Redeemer?
How kind God is! He sent His Son into this world

to be our Savior and He let many pious people see and know the Savior even while He was still a little Child. Just to tell you this story of the Child Jesus makes me, too, feel happy.

What did the holy old man, Simeon, do when the Holy Ghost put into his mind that the Child in holy Mary's arms was the Savior? What did he say to God? How happy he was that the Savior had come. He was ready to die just because he had seen the Savior. What did holy Anna do so gladly because she saw the Savior? So you must be happy when I tell you about Jesus. You must thank God that He has sent His Son into this world.

Oral Completion Test

1. When God whispered to Simeon to go to church, Simeon . . . .

2. When God whispers something to me, I ought to . . . .

Practical

Application

Children, wasn't that good of Simeon to go to church as soon as God whispered to him? If he had not gone, he would not have seen the Savior. See! it is always best to do right away what God puts into your mind. Now when I tell you to pray nicely to God, what should you do? When I tell you to pay attention and study hard, what should you do? When God whispers to you to be obedient at home to your parents, what should you do? Children, everything good that we hear and everything good that enters our mind comes from God. So we must quickly do all those good things that come into our mind. That makes God pleased with us. That shows that we really love God.

Liturgical

How happy Simeon must have been when holy Mary let him take the Child Jesus in his arms! Perhaps you think that only big people can come so close to Jesus. That is not so. Listen now to the story of a little boy to whom Jesus came very close.[3]

This little boy's name was Gerard. He is a great saint in heaven now, so we call him St. Gerard. When Gerard was still a small boy of three or four years, he liked to go to church. He would kneel there all alone and pray to Jesus in the tabernacle. He used to tell his mother that he did not want little Jesus to be lonely.

One day Gerard came home from church with a tiny loaf of bread. His mother, of course, asked

---

[3]Adapted from *True Stories for First Communicants,* by a Sister of Notre Dame, pp. 14–17.

him where he got it. He told her that a beautiful
lady in the church had given it to him. Gerard's
sister wanted to know who the beautiful lady was,
so one day she followed Gerard to church. She was
surprised to see her little brother stop in front of a
statue of holy Mary with the Infant Jesus. Gerard
looked up at the statue and said: "Come down,
Little One. Here I am." Then a wonderful thing
happened. The holy Child Jesus was standing at
the side of Gerard and when his sister looked up at
the statue she saw holy Mary's arms empty. Jesus
kissed her little brother and talked to him. Then,
giving him a little white loaf of bread, He once
more returned to holy Mary's arms.

What a happy boy Gerard was, you say. Yes,
children, but some day you can be just as happy
as Gerard. Do you know what day that will be?
On your First Communion day, the priest will take
Jesus from His little house on the altar and will
put Him on your tongue. (*Show the picture of a
Child's Communion.*) Then you can take Him into
your heart. Jesus will talk to you, as He did to
Gerard, and you can talk to Him.

Thanksgiving After Communion

Religious		Whenever good children receive Jesus into their
Practice hearts in Holy Communion, they have a lot to tell

Jesus and Jesus has a lot to tell them. They stay
in church some time even after the priest leaves the
altar and pray to Jesus. They are happy to keep
Jesus company.

Dramatize the story of St. Gerard, just previously
told. Emphasize the point of keeping Jesus com- *Activity*
pany when He comes. Have the children make up
little sentences which they imagine Gerard ad-
dressed to Jesus. These self-made prayers would
make excellent material for the children's thanks-
giving after Holy Communion.

Act of Hope

O my God! I hope that You will give me
    what I need today and till I die.   *Prayer*
I hope that You will let me see You
    and be with You forever in heaven.

You will not fail to notice that the following points
are repeatedly emphasized: (1) the feeling of reverence
for Jesus; (2) complete readiness, born of love, to be   *Remarks*
ever obedient to God. By means of this feeling of deep
reverence toward Jesus, the solid foundation of faith
is laid. Without reverence, no amount of future argu-
ment or proof will ever engender faith. By instilling a
spirit of ready obedience to God, faith becomes a living, active force in the child's heart. Reverence and
obedience must always be treated together, for one
without the other would remain sterile. Mere reverence
without obedience is cold and lifeless; while obedience
without reverence is simply impossible.

Part Three

JESUS AT TWELVE

Pictures

Jesus at Twelve (Schumacher)

Devices   The Home at Nazareth (Schumacher)

Introduction

Jesus did not always remain a Baby. Every year
Procedure He grew bigger and bigger. A little while ago I
spoke to you about Jesus, our little Brother. Now
He is Jesus, our big Brother. As our big Brother
He shows us how we ought to act when we grow
up. He shows us especially how we ought to obey
and how we ought to pray.

Where Jesus lived the grown-up people had to go
to the church at Jerusalem three times a year on certain feast days. They came from all over the country to the city of Jerusalem. St. Joseph and holy
Mary used to go there too. They used to take the
Boy Jesus with them. When Jesus was twelve years
old, they went with Him on such a journey to
Jerusalem. Usually a large number of people went
together, as we do in a procession. The children
sometimes kept together by themselves and sometimes they went with their relatives and friends.

Listen to the story of what happened to Jesus when He went to the church in Jerusalem at the time He was twelve years old.

Presentation

When the feast days were over, everyone started back for home. Joseph and Mary had traveled a whole day from Jerusalem. At night they stopped to rest. But Jesus was not with them. They thought He might be somewhere with friends. The next morning they looked for Him among all the people they knew, but Jesus could not be found. By this time they began to worry about Him. So they went all the way back to Jerusalem to look for their dear Jesus. He had been lost three days already. At last they went to the church. There they found their Child. (*Show the picture.*) He was sitting with the teachers. He was listening carefully to what they said, He was asking them questions, and answering any questions that they asked Him. Everyone was looking at Jesus in wonder because He was giving such good answers.

Holy Mary was happy when she saw her dear Son again. Then she said to Him: "My Son, why did You do this to us? Your father and I have worried much because You were lost."

Jesus answered. "Why did you look for Me?

Didn't you know that I must be busy about My Father's work?"

But the Holy Child Jesus was obedient. At once He went back with His mother, Mary, and St. Joseph to their home at Nazareth. There He obeyed them in all things. (*Show the picture.*) Every day as He grew older people could see more and more how bright He was. God the Father in heaven and all the good people who saw Him loved Him each day more and more. Jesus stayed there in Nazareth with His parents until He was thirty years old.

Recapitulation

What a beautiful story of the Child Jesus we have just heard! Can you tell it to me, children? What did the grown-up people who lived long ago have to do three times a year? Where did they have to go? Where did the good St. Joseph and holy Mary go? Where did they take the Boy Jesus? What were they going to do there? How old was Jesus then?

Where did Mary and Joseph go when the feast days were over? Where were the children in such processions? When Jesus was not with His parents, where did they think He was at first? At night the children used to stay with their parents. But where did Jesus stay? What did Mary and Joseph do

when their Boy, Jesus, did not come? And when
they could not find Him among their friends, to
what city did they go to look for Him? Where did
they at last find Him in Jerusalem? What was He
doing there? How was He listening to the teachers?
How did He answer when they asked Him questions? Did He go back home gladly with His parents? How was He at home when Joseph or Mary
told Him to do anything?

The Child in Church, in School, and at Home

Children, where do your good parents go on Sun-
days and Holydays? Why do they go to church? *Application*
They take you with them as long as you are little.
See! the Boy Jesus was glad to go to church with
His parents. He went there to hear about God, to
speak about God, and to pray to Him. So you
should be glad to go to church with your parents.
Make up your mind to listen nicely to what you
hear about God in church. Make up your mind to
pray well to God.

When Mary and Joseph found Jesus He was
talking to the teachers. Where do you talk to your
teachers? Here in school you also hear about God
and you can ask questions about God.

Now there was one other place where Jesus liked
to be. Can you tell me that place? Yes, at home

with His parents. After they found Him, Jesus went back home with them and did everything they told Him. Like Jesus, you should be happy at home with your parents. And like Jesus, you should obey your parents always.

What did Jesus answer holy Mary when she told Him that she was so worried while· He was lost? "You didn't have to look for Me," He said. "You should have known that I would be busy about My Father's work." Who is that Father of Whom Jesus spoke? Yes, it is God. Do you remember yet that the Angel Gabriel said Jesus would be the Son of God? Now Jesus Himself calls God His Father. Jesus Christ, our Lord and Savior, is the Son of God. Children, love and please good Jesus, the Son of God. Be happy to be with Him in church and be glad to hear what the priest tells you there about Him. Listen very quietly on Sunday morning when the priest talks to you about Jesus. Remember that Jesus Himself is watching you from His little house on the altar. Be glad, too, to be in school, especially when your teacher tells you stories about Jesus. When you pay attention in school, you make Jesus happy. Also please Jesus, the Son of God, when you are at home by always obeying your parents.

Children, tell me once more the three places where you should be glad to be. Try to act in these

three places like Jesus acted. Promise now that you
will try. Say with me: "Good Jesus, I will try to
pray in church like You prayed. I will try to listen
closely in school as You wish me to do. I will try
to obey at home as You obeyed. Jesus, Son of God,
I want to please You." (*Repeat.*)

Act of Love

> O my God! I love You with all my heart,
>> because You are so good, and so kind to me.
> I will love other people as myself,
>> because You want me to.

Prayer

Little hymns, appropriate to this period in the
life of Jesus and appropriate for First Holy Communion, could be learned.

Religious Practice

For this unit we would suggest activities cen-
tered about the classroom Crib. The star and the
Three Wise Men could be put in place for the first
part of the unit. Little childlike prayers and devotions to Jesus in the Crib, expressing especially desire to receive Him, could be suited to part two.
For part three, the figure of Jesus could be taken
from the Manger. Let the children express the sorrow of Mary and Joseph, of the angels, of the shepherds and of the Three Wise Men over the loss of
Jesus. Losing Jesus through serious sin could be
made the application.

Culminating Activity

Remarks   Only those events in the Life of Jesus are presented·
to these young children, which are calculated especially
to incite deep reverence toward the Savior and thus
lay the foundation of faith, and those which show in
bold outline the course of divine revelation. Accordingly, the story of the murder of the Holy Innocents,
the flight into Egypt, and the return have been omitted
in these instructions for the little ones. The story of
the Child Jesus at the age of twelve was considered
necessary, since it shows the venerable character of
Jesus and since the lesson of obedience can be so well
instilled in these children through the example of Jesus'
Childhood.

In our succeeding instructions, many events in the
Life of Jesus will be passed over. The following objectives will guide our selection: (1) to present the chief
doctrines of the Catholic Faith; (2) to impress upon
the child's mind our entire dependence upon God and
His fatherly care of us; (3) to make the child see that
obedience to God should spring not merely from a sense
of obligation, but rather from a motive of gratitude
and humility.

These same objectives will also guide us in the selection of the details presented in these stories. Reverence toward Jesus, spiritual joy in knowing Him, readiness to believe in Him, and willingness to follow His
example, must be our guiding principles in the choice
of story material. Especially the last named, willingness
to follow the example of Jesus, must be brought to the
fore in all our instructions to little children. In God's
plan of restoring the fallen human race, the example
of Christ was to play an all-important part. Thus the

Church prays in the Preface of the Mass on Christmas Day, that since we know God in visible form we may be carried through Jesus to the love of invisible things. For this reason, the following features in the story of the twelve-year-old Boy Jesus have been emphasized: Jesus liked to be in church, He liked to be with the teachers, and with His parents. No attempt was made to give a description of the temple, the temple-school, or of the Jewish feast days. Things were considered only in their religious and moral aspect, and not with an eye to historical accuracy.

UNIT SIX

Content

1. Jesus is Baptized in the Jordan.
2. Jesus Shows His Wonder-Working Powers.

Objectives

1. To follow Jesus in His public life and to grow in reverence toward Him.

2. To build up our faith in and our love of Him by seeing His power and His goodness to men.

3. To realize that adoration and petition can be made to our Eucharistic Savior the same as when He lived visibly in the flesh.

Part One

JESUS IS BAPTIZED IN THE JORDAN

Pictures

Jesus Baptized by John (Schumacher)
Symbol of the Blessed Trinity — Shamrock   *Devices*

Introduction

Children, so far I have been telling you stories
of the Infant Jesus and of the little Boy Jesus. But *Procedure*
Jesus did not always stay small. He grew to be a
Man just as any other boy. I am going to tell you
what Jesus did when He was a Man.

Presentation

When Jesus was thirty years old He began to
teach. He taught about God. He taught what God
wants us to do and what He will give us. He said
that God will make us happy forever and ever, if
we really love Him and are really obedient to Him.
Jesus told us, too, how ready God is to help us be
good, because we cannot be good alone. We cannot
be good alone, because the sin of Adam and Eve
made us weak and bad.

121

Before Jesus began to teach, there was a very holy and pious man, named John, who started to preach. He begged the people to be good. He said they should try to be good, because the Redeemer of men, the Savior, was coming soon. Some of the people promised to be better when they heard John. They told him they would stop doing bad things and start doing what was good and right. John had these people stand in the river and poured water over them as a sign that they wanted their souls to be washed from sin. You call that baptizing. So John is called John the Baptist.

Jesus also came to John. The soul of Jesus was, of course, very, very pure. He did not have to be better. Still He let John baptize Him. When Jesus stepped out of the water after His baptism, He was praying. Suddenly the heavens above opened up and the Holy Ghost in the form of a dove came upon Him. At the same time a voice called down from heaven: "You are My dear Son; I am very well pleased with You." (*Show the picture.*)

Recapitulation

What did Jesus do when He was thirty years old? To whom did He go first? What did John do? What did he preach to the people? Some of the people promised him to be better. What did he do to them in the water? What name do we give to John because he baptized the people? What did Jesus do there with John the Baptist? What happened when Jesus was baptized? Who came down upon Him? Whose voice was heard from heaven? What did the voice say? What did God call Jesus? Whose Son is Jesus? Yes, Jesus is God's Son. God is His Father. Do you still remember what the Angel Gabriel told holy Mary about the Child 'she would receive? Whose Son would He be? The twelve-year-old Jesus Himself said to His Mother Mary: "Why did you look for Me. Didn't you know that I must be busy about My Father's work?" And Who came upon Jesus in the form of a dove?

Doctrinal

See! dear children, there are three Persons in God: the Father, the Son, and the Holy Ghost. *Application* Whose voice was heard from heaven? What did God the Father say of Jesus? Who is Jesus, then? And Who came upon Jesus, the Son of God, in the form of a dove?

So there are these three Persons in God: the Father, the Son, and the Holy Ghost. Whenever we make the sign of the cross, we use the name of the three Persons in God and we say that we believe in them. We say: In the name of the Father, and of the Son, and of the Holy Ghost. There is only one God, but in that one God there are three Persons. (*Show the symbol of the Blessed Trinity.*)

How many Persons are there in God? What do we call them? But these three Persons are only one God. We have only one God. Is there more than one God? But how many Persons are there in God? Tell me their names. As often as you make the sign of the cross, you must think of God. When you say "In the name of the Father," think of God the Father. When you say, "And of the Son," think of God the Son, Who is Jesus Christ. When you say, "And of the Holy Ghost," think of God the Holy Ghost. We believe in one God. But we believe in three Persons in that one God, the Father, the Son, and the Holy Ghost.

Liturgical — Confession

Children, what did God the Father say about Jesus? He said: "You are My dear Son; I am very well pleased with You." Did God ever say anything like that about us? Yes, at our baptism, He said: "You are now My child. I am well pleased with you." God said that because after baptism our soul was very pure. Jesus' Soul, of course, was very, very pure even before His baptism. Our soul is pure only after our baptism.

Suppose now that we dirty our soul with sin after our baptism. Can we clean it again? Yes, by being sorry for our sins and going to confession. God takes away all sin from our souls if we are really sorry and tell our sins to the priest. God loves us very much after we have made a good confession, because then our soul is pure.

When you want Jesus to come into your heart, you must be very pure. Your soul must be clean. Sin, you know, dirties your soul. If you have some big dirty spots on your soul, some big sins, what must you do before Jesus comes into your heart? Yes, make a good confession. When you are really sorry for those sins and tell them to the priest, God wipes them from your soul. Then your soul is clean and pure. Jesus is glad to come into your heart if your soul is clean and pure.

Repetition of the two forms of the sign of the *Religious Practice* cross together with the words.

Drawing for the religion booklet: a shamrock — *Activity* adding "God."

Part Two

JESUS SHOWS HIS WONDER-
WORKING POWERS

Pictures

Devices   Jesus Cures the Sick (Schumacher)

Introduction

Who will tell us how old Jesus was when He
Procedure left His Mother and His home in Nazareth? What
did Jesus do after He left home? What wonderful
thing happened after Jesus was baptized? Now children, we will go on with our story.

Presentation

Jesus left John the Baptist and went off into a
lonely place where no one lived. There He did not
eat or drink anything for forty days and nights. He
prayed, too, during all that time. Afterwards He
came out of this lonely place. Then He walked
about in the country of the Jews. He preached
everywhere. Wherever He went, He did good things
for the people.

Later on, I shall tell you about the holy things
the dear Jesus taught us about God. I hope you will

pay close attention to what Jesus asks us to do. I hope you will do it, too. Oh! if Jesus were only here with us now, so that we could see and hear Him! Or if we had been living then, and could have seen Him and heard Him talk! How happy we would have been! But some of the things Jesus taught are written down in a big book. Some other things that Jesus taught are known to us, too, because those who heard them told other people and they told still others. So these words of Jesus have come down to us.

Children, the great, good Jesus did so many kind deeds for men while He lived on earth. Just to hear about these deeds makes us happy. When we have finished listening to them, we must say: "No man can do such things; only God, the Son of God, can do them."

Today, I shall tell you only a few of the kind deeds Jesus did to help poor sick people. He didn't have to give them any pills or any medicine. One day, when a blind man asked Jesus to make him see, Jesus just spoke a few words. At once the blind man could see. Another time Jesus touched His hand to the eyes of two blind men. They could see right away. Still another time, Jesus met a man who had been born blind. Jesus mixed some spittle and dirt, rubbed it over the man's eyes, and sent him to a pool of water where he was to wash his eyes. While the blind man was washing his eyes, they were suddenly opened. He could see. He had never seen anything in his whole life before, but now he could see. (*Show a picture illustrating one or the other of these miracles.*)

People who were deaf and dumb were also helped by Jesus. Deaf people are those who cannot hear; dumb people are those who cannot talk. Jesus opened the ears of the deaf and loosened the tongues of the dumb. All He had to do was to will it. One day, Jesus put His finger into the ears of a deaf man, touched the man's tongue with spittle, looked up to heaven to His Father, and said to the man: "May your ears be opened and may your tongue be loosened." At once the man was able to hear and talk.

Lame persons, who were not able to walk even one step, were brought to Jesus on their beds. The kind and great Jesus helped them. Once Jesus said to one of these lame men: "Stand up! Carry your bed and go home!" The lame man got right up and was able to walk. (*Show picture.*)

Recapitulation

Children, these are wonderful stories you have just heard. After Jesus had fasted forty days and nights, He went about the country of the Jews. He taught the people what God wanted them to do, and He did many great things for poor sick people. What did He do one day for a man who had been born blind? How did He cure the man who was deaf and dumb? Tell me how He made the lame man get up from his bed and walk. Did Jesus need any medicine to cure these sick people? How long did it take Him to cure them? How great Jesus is! How kind to poor sick people!

Oral Completion Test

1. The blind were made to see, the deaf to hear, the lame to walk, as quickly as Jesus . . . . . .

2. When Jesus worked these wonders, He showed that He is . . . . . . and . . . . . .

Doctrinal

Children, see what great things Jesus did to help poor sick people! How fine it would be, if Jesus *Application* were living here now as He lived long ago, and we could see these wonders! How great if we could watch Jesus make the blind man see, the deaf man hear, the dumb man talk, the lame man get up from his bed and walk! How we would wonder and say: "Jesus can do everything He wills; He is so good He wants to help everyone!" If we had heard

Jesus preach, we should have believed everything
He said. If He had told us to do something, we
should have done it at once.

Yes, children, at the time Jesus lived on earth,
the good people who saw these wonderful things
said that Jesus must have come from God. They
believed in Him. The man who was born blind and
who was cured by Jesus told the people: "No one
ever heard of any man who could make a person
born blind like me see all at once. If this Jesus did
not come from God, He could not have done that."
When Jesus cured the deaf-and-dumb man, all those
who were standing around cried out: "He does all
things well: He makes the deaf to hear, and the
dumb to speak."

Children, we too will believe in the dear Jesus
Who did so many great things. We will obey Him
in all things that He teaches us. We will do whatever our teacher tells us that Jesus wants.

Liturgical

This great, good Jesus Who worked so many
wonders is still living. He lives in that little house
on the altar. We cannot see Him like the people
did long ago. But we know He is there, for He has
told us so. Perhaps we would like the great, good
Jesus to help us, too, just as He helped the people

long ago. We are only children, but Jesus loves children and He wants to help them out of their little troubles. If we wish Jesus to help us, we must go to Him and beg His help. We know where He lives, so we will go to Him and tell Him what we need. Some day soon, Jesus will come very near to you; yes, He will come into your very hearts. Then you can say to Him: "You are the good Jesus, Who made the blind man see. Help me to believe in You. You are the good Jesus, Who made the dumb man talk. Help me to love You and pray to You. You are the good Jesus, Who made the lame man walk. Help me to follow You."

Teach some simple hymn to Jesus in the Blessed Sacrament.   *Hymn*

For this unit we would suggest that the children cut out pictures of Jesus the Savior and paste them in their religion booklet. Teach the children to be reverent with these holy pictures. Short sentences might be written by the children beneath these pictures. The following are suggestive: Jesus, I believe in You. Jesus, I love You. Jesus, I will do what You want.   *Culminating Activity*

The purpose of the stories of this Unit is to instill faith through the feeling of reverence. From this follows necessarily the acknowledgment of man's lowliness and the duty of submitting to the teaching of Jesus.   *Remarks*

Little children may not be able to retain all these

stories. That, of course, is not the object at this period
in their lives. They will hear them again in later years
more in detail and then they will remember them better
and understand them more clearly. The object now is to
instill deep reverence toward Jesus because of His power
and His goodness to mankind. Out of this reverence
will grow a firm faith and an ardent love. These two
constitute the essence of religion of the heart. These
feelings will abide with the children even after the details of the stories have been forgotten.

UNIT SEVEN

Content

1. Jesus' Teaching on the Love of God.
2. Jesus' Teaching on the Love of our Neighbor.
3. His Lesson on the Immortality of the Soul.
4. His Lesson on the Resurrection of the Body.
5. Friends and Enemies of Jesus' Teaching.

Objectives

1. To know in childlike form the Commandments of God.

2. To know what to do in the confessional.

3. To realize that there is a reward awaiting the child that follows the teaching of Jesus and also a punishment for the child that does not.

4. To picture those that take sides with Jesus and those that are against Him: and to line ourselves up with those who are for Him.

Part One

JESUS' TEACHING ON THE LOVE OF GOD

Pictures

God (the three Persons) and His Creation
A Child in the Confessional   *Devices*

Introduction

Jesus preached everywhere throughout the land
of the Jews. Oftentimes very many people used to *Procedure*
gather about Him to hear His beautiful teaching.
The good people were very happy when they could
listen to Him. They believed His holy words. But
the bad people did not want to believe Him, because they wanted to stay bad. Listen now and I
shall tell you some of the things Jesus taught.

Presentation

1. God loves men more than anyone can imagine.
He loved them so much that He gave them His only
Son, Jesus Himself. All who believe in Jesus will
not be lost; they will receive life forever (John 6,
40).

God loves men as a good father loves his children (Matt. 6, 9). That is why you should pray to Him: Our Father, Who art in heaven. Yes, God loves all men. Like a good father, He gives them what they need if they lead good lives and work hard. A good person who works hard and lives a holy life does not have to worry. God will surely give him what he needs. Jesus one day said: "Do not worry and ask, 'What shall we eat? what shall we wear?' Look at the birds. They do not plant seeds nor do they gather up their food into a barn. Still your Father in heaven feeds them. You are worth more than they are. God loves you more than He loves them. Why should you worry about the clothes you are to wear? Look at the flowers in the field. See how they grow. They do not work and still they are clothed in more beautiful colors than even a great king. Now, if God gives such fine clothes even to the grass, how much more will He do for you! (Matt. 6, 25 ff.) Your Father in heaven knows before you ask that you need things to eat and wear. Just be careful about being good and pious. Everything you need will be given to you. Whatever you ask the Father in My Name, He will give you" (John 15, 16).

(*Repeat in question form.*) What did Jesus teach about God? How is God toward us? Like what?

Your father loves you. If you ask him for something that is good for you, does he give it to you? But your father is not always able to give you everything, even if he would like to. Jesus said to us: God is like a good father. Just as your father wants to give you nice things, so does God also. And God has all things. He can give you anything He wants to. Because He loves you like a good father, He will give you everything you need. See, how many things the kind Father in heaven gives us! (*Show the picture of Creation.*) He never stops giving. Who makes us live? Who lets all things grow that we need to eat? Who created the water we need when we are thirsty? Who created the things from which our clothes are made? Everything, yes, everything we have received from the dear, good God. He loves us like a kind, rich father. What did Jesus teach us to call God? How should we pray to Him?

2. The dear, good God is our Father in heaven. He loves us so much. We should love Him too. It would be terrible if we did not love Him.

Jesus teaches us that this is the first and the greatest commandment — to love God. One time a certain man asked Jesus: "Master, which is the greatest commandment?" Jesus answered: "You shall love the Lord your God with your whole soul and with your whole mind and heart" (Matt. 22,

37–38). This is the first and the greatest commandment.

(*Repeat in question form.*) Children! Who made all of us? Who keeps us and cares for us every second? Who is very kind to us and gives us everything we need? Who gives you your parents and your teachers? Who sent us Jesus, our Savior? This is the kind God Who loves us so much. Jesus tells us to love this good God. How much should we love Him? Should we be glad to think of God? pray to Him? do everything that pleases Him? stay away from everything that He forbids? We should not love this good God half and half. How much, does Jesus say? Not with half a heart, half a soul. With how much of our heart? how much of our soul? Should we also love bad things a little? How then should we love God?

3. Yes, children, that is the way it should be. We must love God with our whole soul, our whole mind, our whole heart. Now listen again to Jesus. He says: "Only that person who does as My Father in heaven commands will enter the kingdom of heaven" (Matt. 7, 21). What did Jesus mean? He meant this: It does not help if we say to God, "I love You," but do not do what He wants of us. We must do what He tells us. We must do it because

we love Him. We must do it because **He** wants it.
That is the only way to show that we love God.
That is the way to keep the first and the greatest
commandment. Where does Jesus promise that we
will go then?

Recapitulation

Now let me see how much you remember of what
I have told you today. When Jesus began to preach,
about Whom did He speak to the people? How does
God deal with all people? How should they pray to
God? What will God surely give them here on
earth? As He takes care of the birds and the flowers,
so He will take care of us. But we have to work,
we have to live good lives, we have to do what is
right. Then we will get what we need from God.
Whom did God send to us because He loved us so
much? Those who believe in Jesus will not be lost.
But those who do not believe in Him will be lost.
Those who believe in Him will receive life forever
in heaven. Yes, children, God loves us very much.
So we, too, ought to love this good God. How much?
We should try with our whole heart to love Him.
We should try to please Him with our whole soul.
How do you show that you love God? What did
Jesus say? What commandment is this?

Oral Completion Test

1. God loves us as a good . . . . . .

2. God loved us so much that He sent us the . . . . . .

3. We show that we love God by doing what He . . . . . .

Application   1. Dear children, whenever you look at anything, you should think to yourself: the good Father in heaven gives me that. When you see a little bird flying about with a seed or worm or leaf in its mouth, or when you see a little bird eating one of these, do you know Who takes care of that bird? Then you should think to yourself: If God takes care of the birds, He will also take care of me. For God is our Father. Out in the field, there are many beautiful flowers — red, white, yellow, and blue flowers. When you look at them, do you know Who made them so beautiful? Then you can say to yourself: If God takes care of the flowers of the field, He will take still more care of me. For God is our Father.

Of course, when we need something we must ask God for it, just as the child must ask its father. If we ask Him, and if we are good and obedient, then He will give it to us. What great promise did Jesus make to us? "If you ask the Father in My Name, you will receive what you ask for." How good God is! How good Jesus is! Through Jesus we can get everything. Through Him we will be made happy forever.

2. Jesus promised us something very great. Let us promise Him something, too. Let us promise that we will keep this first and greatest commandment. But to love God, you must be obedient to Him. Tell me what God wants a little child to do. What does a little child owe to God? (*Draw out from the children the chief duties they owe to God — first three commandments.*) God wants you to pray to Him — when? where? Where does God want you to go on Sunday? What does God want you to do on Friday?

(*The following sentences might be put on the blackboard or better on flash cards of varied colors. The manner of confessing the sins against these commandments should be rehearsed here.*)

GOD WANTS US TO PRAY.

GOD WANTS US TO SPEAK HIS NAME WITH LOVE.

GOD WANTS US TO GO TO MASS ON SUNDAY.

GOD WANTS US NOT TO EAT MEAT ON FRIDAY.

A Visit to the Confessional

(*First show the children a picture of a child in the confessional. Explain briefly. Then take them*   **Religious Practice**

into the church and show them the confessional.)
There in the center, children, is where the priest
will be. The priest takes the place of God. Now
look in here at the side. See the crucifix hanging
there! That reminds you that Jesus died for your
sins. You should be sorry that you hurt Jesus so
much. When you go in there, you kneel down. I
shall tell you in a few moments what prayers you
say in the confessional. Then you tell the priest
your sins, not too loud and not too still, just so
the priest can hear them. The priest in the confessional has the power of Jesus. He can take away
your sins. When the priest speaks the words that
Jesus told him to speak, all your sins are washed
from your soul by the Blood of Jesus. O Jesus, how
good You are to take away my sins! O Jesus, how
good You are to give me the confessional!

*(When the children return to the classroom, they
might learn these key sentences about their visit to
the confessional.)*

TODAY I SAW THE CONFESSIONAL — WHERE I
TELL GOD MY SINS.

TODAY I SAW THE CONFESSIONAL — WHERE GOD
TAKES AWAY MY SINS.

TODAY I SAW THE CONFESSIONAL — WHERE GOD
MAKES ME A GOOD CHILD.

Before and After Confession

Prayer for help to make a good confession.

Sign of the cross. Bless me, Father. This is my *Prayers* first confession. . . .

I am sorry for all my sins.

Motto cards may be made by cutting and arranging the letters. Suggestions: "God is Good," "Jesus *Activity* Help Me," "Go to Mass on Sunday."[1]

Part Two

JESUS' TEACHING ON THE LOVE OF OUR NEIGHBOR

Pictures

The Good Samaritan (Schumacher)
Jesus Feeding the Multitude   *Devices*

Introduction

Children, when Jesus was asked which is the greatest commandment, He answered: "You shall *Procedure* love the Lord your God with your whole soul and with your whole mind and heart. This is the first

---

[1]*Correlation of Art and the Mass,* by Joseph Reiner, S.J., and Eunice Foster (Chicago: Practical Drawing Company, 1931), pp. 17, 18.

and the greatest commandment." Now who will tell
us some ways in which we can show our love for
God? Yes, but Jesus did not only tell the people to
love God. He told them something else too. Just
listen to what He told them.

Presentation

1. Just as soon as Jesus had finished saying "This
is the first and the greatest commandment," He
said: "The second commandment is like the first.
You shall love your neighbor as yourself" (Matt.
22, 39).

The good, dear God is the Father of all men. He
loves them all as His children. He wants them to
live together as good children of one and the same
Father. Now listen closely! You, and you, and you,
have brothers and sisters at home. How does your
good Daddy want you to live together? Does he
like it when you quarrel and fight among yourselves? Is he pleased when Mary becomes angry
because sister gets a fine new dress? Is he pleased
when one of his children always wants the others
to give in and do things his way?

Is Daddy happy when brothers and sisters get
along well together? when John does something to
please Mary? when Betty is glad that Rita got
something nice from Mother? when all are sad if

brother or sister is sick? when all want the sick one to get better and are anxious to do something to please the little patient in bed?

Now listen again very closely! God is the Father of all people. He gives life to all. He wants them all to get along well. So He wishes one person to help the other. He wants them to think of one another and to act toward one another as His children. When I look at you, dear children, at each one of you, I think to myself: each one of you is a child of God, just as I am, too. I and all of you belong to the dear God. We all are His children. I feel so happy when I look at you and think of that. Then I think again to myself; the good God is pleased if I am good to you, His children. He would not be pleased if I were not ready to do kind things to His children, who are my brothers and sisters.

You, too, dear children, must think to yourselves: all people are the children of God. He is their kind Father, just as He is my kind Father. I must love all people because God is their Father.

When Jesus said that you must love your neighbor as you love yourself, a bad man asked Him: "Yes, but who is my neighbor?" In answer, Jesus told him this story:

A Jew was traveling from one city to another. On the way he was held up by robbers. The robbers stole everything he had with him. Then they hit him so hard that he fell down, and lay there, half dead, in his own blood. The robbers ran away. Some time later, a Jewish priest came along the same way. He saw the poor man lying there, covered with blood, but he passed by without helping him. A little later, another Jew went by. He also looked at the poor man, but kept on his way. Finally, a stranger came along the same road. The stranger was not a Jew. But when he saw the poor man lying wounded in his own blood, he went up to him. He felt very sorry for this poor man. So he poured wine and oil on his wounds and bandaged them up. (*Show picture.*) Then he took the poor man on his donkey and brought him to a hotel and cared for him there. But the stranger had to travel on, so he gave the hotel keeper some money and said to him: "Take good care of this man; if it costs more money than I gave you, I will pay you more when I come back."

Then Jesus said to the bad man who asked Him the question: "Who acted like a neighbor to this poor man who was robbed and hurt — the Jewish priest, the second Jew, or the stranger?" (Luke 10, 30 ff.) Now children, I am going to ask you this same question: who acted like a neighbor? Did the Jewish priest, who was not sorry for the poor man, even though he was a Jew like himself, and did not help him, but just passed by? Did the second Jew act like a neighbor? Or did the stranger who felt sorry and helped? Even that bad man who asked Jesus the question had to answer: "The stranger, who helped, acted like a neighbor." Jesus then said to him: "Do the same thing. Help him who needs help, even if you do not know him, because he is a child of God just as you are."

(*Repeat in question form.*) Now children, Jesus wants us to love God, doesn't He? Whom else must we love? Who are our neighbors? How many people? Why must we love all people? Who loves them all as a Father? Whose children are they all? Yes, God's children. That is why we must love them all. When things go well with them, we should be happy. When they get hurt or some other evil happens to them, how should we feel? What should we do if we can? God is pleased with us if we love His children.

2. Listen to what Jesus said further: "Whatever you want people to do to you, do also to them" (Matt. 7, 12). What did Jesus say we should do to other people? What shouldn't we do to them? When you fall and hurt yourself, you want someone to help you. If you see someone hurt himself, and you are able to help him, then you should help

him. You want someone to give you a piece of
bread if you are hungry. So if you see a hungry
child, and you happen to have a piece of bread,
give that hungry child some of your bread. You do
not like anyone to hit you. So you must not hit anyone either. You do not like to have anyone take
your things away. You must not take others' things
away either. You do not like others to laugh at
you when you make a mistake. Do not laugh at
them when they make a mistake. You must do to
others as you want them to do to you.

Recapitulation

What is the second commandment that Jesus tells
us to keep? It is as great as the first commandment
which tells us to love God. How many people are
our neighbors? Why must we love all people? If
we love them all because they are the children of
God, how will our Father in heaven feel? Is it right
for us not to love someone? What is such a person?
Yes, a child of God, and our Father in heaven is
not pleased if we do not love one of His children.
How did Jesus say we should love our neighbor?
How much should we love them all? Yes, this is
what He said: What you wish people to do to you,
you should do to them. Our heart hurts when we
have to suffer something. How must our heart feel

when we see someone else suffering? We want others to help us in our troubles. So when we see someone in trouble, what should we do if we are able? We are glad when things go well with us. How should we feel when things go well with others? We do not like anyone to take things from us that make us happy. So we should not take things from them that make them happy. If we love God and love all men like that for the sake of God, God will be pleased with us.

Children, if you would only love all people that way, you would be following the dear Jesus. He *Application* loved all people. He was sorry when He saw someone suffer. He helped them when they needed help. You still remember how He made blind people see, deaf people hear, dumb people talk, and lame people walk. He did all these things because He loved these poor people. Jesus especially loved children. Often the mothers brought their children to Jesus. They wanted Him to pray over their little ones. And Jesus did. He laid His hands on their heads and prayed over them. One day, you remember, the disciples did not want to let the children come to the Savior. But Jesus said: "Let the little children come to Me!" (Mark 10, 14.)

Now I want to tell you a story to show you how Jesus felt sorry for poor people who needed help.

Jesus often used to stay in places where no people lived. But even there, good men and women and children would follow Him to hear His teaching. One day there was a crowd of over 5,000 people listening to Jesus in one of these places. (*Show picture.*) Toward evening Jesus told His good Apostles to give them something to eat. But there was no food there, except five loaves of bread and two fishes. Jesus told them to bring Him the bread and fishes. He turned His eyes to heaven, prayed over the bread, broke the loaves, and ordered them to be passed around to the people. All the people ate until they were filled. When they had finished, there were still enough little pieces left over to fill twelve baskets (Matt. 14, 15 ff.).

Children, only Jesus can help in this wonderful way, because He is God, the Son of God. But we can learn this lesson from Him. We should be kind to those who need our help, our heart should hurt us when we see someone suffer, and we should help as much as we can.

God wants us to love our neighbor. He wants us to love our parents and to be obedient to them. He wants us to be kind to our brothers and sisters and playmates; not to quarrel or fight with them. He wants us to be honest with all people; not to take things that do not belong to us. He wants us to tell the truth to our parents, teachers, and to all other people; never to tell lies.

Blackboard or Flash Card Summary

(The manner of confessing the sins against these commandments should be rehearsed here.)

GOD WANTS US TO BE KIND AND OBEDIENT TO OUR PARENTS.

GOD WANTS US TO BE KIND TO ALL PEOPLE.

GOD WANTS US TO KEEP OUR SOUL AND BODY PURE.

GOD WANTS US TO BE HONEST WITH ALL PEOPLE.

GOD WANTS US TO TELL THE TRUTH TO ALL PEOPLE.

The story of the good Samaritan is very well suited for dramatization. *Activity*

Give the children some specific act of kindness to practice at home or in school. Point out after it has *Practice* been done how pleasing it was to Jesus. The little ones should be encouraged to give that pleasure often to Jesus.

This and the preceding lesson contain the principal points of Jesus' moral teaching. An effort has been *Remarks* made in these instructions to plant the seed of holy love, the only fruitful seed of true virtue, into the affections and, as far as possible, into the understanding of

the children. The example of Jesus has been used to
stimulate the little ones to imitate the all-holy Model
of regenerated humanity. The miracle of the multiplication of the loaves was cited for a second reason;
namely, to induce the children to accept Jesus' teaching
more readily and to strengthen their faith in Him.

Part Three

JESUS' LESSON ON THE IMMOR-
TALITY OF THE SOUL

Picture

Devices   The Sacred Heart, or Jesus Friend of Children

Chalk Talks
I, p. 22.[2]

Introduction
Now I shall tell you some more of the joyous
Procedure teaching of Jesus Christ. Can you still tell me what
God said would happen to Adam and Eve if they
ate of the forbidden fruit? What really happened
to Adam and Eve after they grew old? Did the disobedience of Adam and Eve hurt anyone besides
themselves? Whom? All of us were born into this

[2]*Chalk Talks I,* by Jerome F. O'Connor, S.J., and William
Hayden, S.J. (St. Louis: Queen's Work Press, 1928).

world with this badness on our souls. What will happen to all of us because of this disobedience? Just as Adam and Eve had to die, so all of us will have to die too. When a person dies, I told you that the soul leaves the body. Today, I am going to tell you what Jesus teaches us about the soul.

Presentation

One day Jesus said to the good people who believed His words: "Do not be afraid of men who can kill your body, but cannot kill your soul. Rather be afraid of the dear God, Who can put your body and soul into hell" (Matt. 10, 28).

Children, do you understand what Jesus meant by these words? He said that men can kill your body, but they cannot kill your soul. The body dies, but the soul does not die. When the body dies, the soul leaves the body and keeps on living. It will live forever, forever, forever.

Do you know where the soul goes when the body dies? Listen and I shall tell you. A real bad soul God will put into hell. Of course, He will not put a good soul into hell. Hear what Jesus says about the souls of good people. A short time before He died, the dear Savior told the good people who were listening to Him: "In My Father's House there are many nice places. I am going there to prepare a place for you. Then I shall come again and take you with Me, that you may be where I am" (John 14, 2–3).

How good of Jesus! His Father's House is heaven. In heaven there are many beautiful places for all good people. Jesus said He was going back to heaven to get these places ready for the good people. Then He said He would come again to take the good people with Him. He wants to have them with Him. Children, you want to be with the dear, good Jesus, don't you? (*Show a picture of the Sacred Heart or a picture of Jesus Friend of Children.*)

Recapitulation

Let us see if you remember this lesson that Jesus taught us. What can men kill? What can't they kill? When the body dies, what does not die? Does God kill the soul? Where does God put a real bad soul? Where does He take a good soul? What did Jesus mean by His Father's House? Where did Jesus go when He died? What did He promise to good people? Where will He take their souls? With Whom will the good people be then? Will they be happy with God the Father and with His Son Jesus? How long will they be happy in heaven? Forever, children! Without end!

Practical

Oh, how good the dear God is! How we should thank Jesus for this lesson today! Think children! *Application* My soul, your soul, will never die. If you really love God as Jesus told you to, then your soul will go to heaven. But you must please God by being obedient to Him. You must love Him with your whole soul and with your whole mind and heart. You must love your neighbor, too, as you love yourself. Remember, your neighbor is God's child. That is why you must love him. Do not wish evil to anyone. Do not do evil to anyone. Be glad when things go well with others. Be ready to help them if you can. Make others happy. Then your soul will go to heaven. It will go to Jesus. You will live forever with Him in heaven. (*Chalk Talks — The Road to Heaven.*)

But not all souls will go to heaven. Not all will go to Jesus. Listen to what Jesus said: "Bad souls, who do not love God and their neighbor, will be put into hell." (*Show the roads leading to hell.*) Children, when you feel like disobeying God or doing evil to your neighbor, oh, then fear God! What did Jesus say God can do? Yes, He will do just what He said to those who do not love Him or their neighbor. How terrible!

Liturgical —· Holy Communion

Dear little children! You have heard something today that should make you very happy. Your soul will never die. It will live forever. If you are good children, your soul will live forever in heaven with God. You want to be good children, don't you? But sometimes you find it very hard to be good. Jesus knows how hard it is for us to be good. So He comes into our heart in Holy Communion to make us strong and help us fight the bad that is in us.

Did you ever watch the priest give Holy Communion to the people who go up to the Communion rail? Before the priest puts the living Body of Jesus on the person's tongue, he makes the sign of the cross while holding Jesus in his fingers. If you listen closely you will hear that the priest is saying something. This is what he says: "May the Body of our Lord Jesus Christ keep your soul for heaven." What a beautiful prayer! Yes, Jesus' Body keeps your soul good and makes it ready to live with Him forever in heaven.

Now I have a story to tell you of a wee little girl, called Nellie.[3] People today call her Little

---

[3] Adapted from *True Stories for First Communicants,* by a Sister of Notre Dame (London: Sands & Co. 1919; St. Louis: B. Herder Book Company).

Nellie of God because she was so holy. When Nellie was just three years old her mother died and she was sent to a convent school kept by the Good Shepherd Sisters. Nellie was the smallest child there, yet she had learned to love Holy God more than many other children who were bigger than she. She knew all about Holy Communion, too, and oftentimes she would ask: "When will Holy God come into my heart? Oh, I am longing for Holy God."

I forgot to tell you, children, that during most of this time little Nellie was sick in bed. She was not able to run and play like the other children. Instead, she had to suffer very great pains. But the little girl was glad to suffer because she loved God.

How she wanted to have Jesus come into her heart! She begged and begged to be allowed to make her First Holy Communion. She was only little more than a baby, but she understood so much about Holy Communion that at last she was told that she could soon receive Jesus. Near her cot the Sisters made an altar to the Infant Jesus, and Nellie would lie for hours looking at it and talking to Holy God. They made her a little white dress, a white veil and wreath, and bought her little white shoes and stockings. "Everything must be very nice for Holy God," said Nellie as she looked on with interest, "and you must put them on me again when He takes me up to heaven."

At last the morning of her First Holy Communion came. Little Nellie was dressed and carried into the chapel. During the Mass she folded her tiny hands and said her baby prayers. At Communion time the priest came down from the altar and placed the Body of Jesus on her tongue. Do you know what words the priest said when he did this? Yes, he said: "May the Body of our Lord Jesus Christ keep your soul for heaven."

Dear little Nellie! She was not going to live much longer. After her First Communion she grew worse and worse. She could not be carried to chapel any more. So the priest had to bring Jesus to her in bed. Each day she grew weaker and weaker, until one Sunday a beautiful angel flew down from heaven for Nellie's soul and took it up with him to Holy God. Little Nellie had loved to have Jesus come to her in Holy Communion and Jesus loved to have little Nellie come to Him in heaven. Jesus kept her soul white and pure for heaven. Children, you, too, want Jesus to come to you and keep your soul white and pure, like little Nellie's, for heaven.

Prayer   Jesus, Jesus come to me! Oh, how much I long for Thee!

Part Four

HIS LESSON ON THE RESURRECTION OF THE BODY

Pictures

Jesus Raises the Daughter of Jaïrus

He brings Back to Life the Young Man of Naim   *Devices*
(Schumacher)

The Resurrection of Lazarus

Introduction

Children, last time you heard the beautiful story
of Little Nellie of Holy God. Not long after she   *Procedure*
received her First Holy Communion, an angel came
to take her soul to God. Do you know what happened to her body after she died? Yes, it was
buried in a little grave in the ground. There her
tiny body began to turn to dust. Some day the
same thing will happen to your body when you
die. But now I have something to tell you about
Jesus that will make you happy again. Listen to
these little stories of how Jesus made three dead
people live again.

Presentation

1. One day a very great man came to Jesus and
said to Him: "Lord, my only daughter, a girl of

twelve years, just died. But come, lay Your hand upon her and she shall live again" (Matt. 9, 18; Luke 8, 41 ff.). Jesus was very kind. He went along with the man. When He reached the house, He found many people crying about the child's bed. Jesus was going to bring the girl back to life. So He first told the people who were crying to go away. "The girl is not dead," Jesus said, "but only sleeping." The people knew that the child was dead, and they laughed at the Savior's words. Jesus knew, too, that the girl was dead. But He stepped up to the bed, took the little girl by the hand, and she stood up. She was alive again and well. (*Show the picture.*)

2. Another time, while Jesus was on one of His journeys, He came to a certain city (Luke 7, 11–16). Near the gate of the city, He met a crowd of people carrying out a dead person to the cemetery. This was a young man, the only son of his mother. The poor woman was now alone in the world, for her husband had died some years before. She was crying bitter tears as she walked behind the dead body of her son. When Jesus saw the weeping mother, He felt sorry for her and said: "Do not cry." Then He told those who were carrying the dead young man to stop. Listen! Jesus speaks. "Young man, I tell you, stand up!" See what has

happened! The dead man rises and begins to talk. Jesus gives him back to his mother. He is alive and well. (*Show picture.*)

3. Children, listen now to the third little story. There was a certain house not far from Jerusalem where Jesus liked to go (John 11, 1 ff.). Two sisters, Mary and Martha, lived there with their good brother Lazarus. One day when Jesus was very far away from this place, a messenger came running to Him from the two sisters. This is what the messenger said: "Lord! Lazarus, whom You love so much, is sick." Jesus answered simply: "This sickness is for the glory of the Son of God." And Jesus stayed two more days in the place where the messenger had come to Him. During this time Lazarus died and was buried. After the two days had passed, Jesus started out for the home of the two sisters. It was a long journey. When Jesus arrived at last, Lazarus had already been in his grave four days. Martha came out to meet Jesus and said: "Dear Lord! if You had been here, my brother would not have died. But I know that God gives You everything You ask of Him." Jesus answered: "Your brother will rise again." "Yes," said Martha, "on the day when all the dead shall rise." Then Jesus spoke: "I can waken the dead and give back life. Do you believe that?" "Yes," replied Martha, "I

believe it, because You are the Son of God Who has come into the world."

Just then the other sister, Mary, came out and knelt at the feet of Jesus, saying: "If You had been here, my brother would not have died." And she began to cry out loud, and the people who were standing about began to cry too. But hush! Jesus speaks: "Take Me to the grave."

The two sisters led the way. At the grave, Jesus ordered the men to lift off the stone. "Lord!" said Martha, "he smells bad, he has been dead four days." "If you believe," answered Jesus, "you shall see the power of God." Then Jesus raised His eyes toward heaven and called into the grave: "Lazarus, come out!" And Lazarus came out at once. He was alive and well. (*Show picture.*)

(*Repeat in question form.*) How many dead people did Jesus bring back to life? Who were they? What did Jesus do to the little girl? What happened when the Savior took her by the hand? What did He do to the young man who was being carried to the cemetery? What happened when He told the young man to stand up? How long was Lazarus dead when Jesus came to his grave? Tell me what Jesus did at the grave of Lazarus. What happened when Jesus called down into his grave? Jesus made these three dead people live again. He called to them and they came back to life again. Jesus can do all things.

4. You remember, children, I told you that all people will die. Their bodies will be buried in the ground. You will die, too. Your body will be buried in the ground. To hear that, makes you sad. But the good, great Jesus has a lesson of joy that He wants you to hear. This is the lesson. The hour will come when all those who are in their graves shall awaken at the call of the Son of God. Then they shall arise from their graves. The good people will arise to live forever with God in heaven; the bad people will arise to go to their punishment in hell forever (John 5, 28–29). We do not know when the hour will come for all bodies to rise from their graves. Jesus did not tell us that. But it will come as soon as the voice of the Son of God calls.

Recapitulation

Children, there were three dead people whom Jesus brought back to life. He touched the dead girl; and she stood up, alive and healthy. He commanded the dead young man, whom they were carrying to the cemetery, to rise; and he arose. He called to Lazarus, whose dead body already began to smell, to come out of his grave; and Lazarus came out, alive and healthy.

What will happen to your body when you die? What did Jesus say about the dead bodies of all people? Yes, they will come out of their graves; they will live again. Who will tell them to come out? Whose voice will call them? When the good people come out of their graves, where will their bodies go? Where will the bodies of the bad people go? Yes, the body belongs just where the soul belongs. Now you see how God can cast both soul and body into hell.

Doctrinal

Application

Children! if we had been there to see Jesus bring the little girl back to life or the dead young man or Lazarus, we should have fallen on our knees and cried out: "Son of God! You can do whatever You want to!" But remember, children, that this same Son of God, Who called the three dead people back to life, will one day do the same for us. He will make our bodies arise from their graves. He will call our souls back to our bodies. Then, if we were good, He will take us, body and soul, along with Him into heaven. In heaven we shall never die again. But He will do this only if we have been good, only if we have loved God and our neighbor. If we have not been good, if we have not loved God and our neighbor, we shall arise for judgment. That means, our bodies shall arise from their graves to go down to punishment in hell forever.

Oh children! we shall ask Jesus often: "Dear Jesus, help us to be good. Help us really to love God, to love You, our Savior, to love our neighbor. Watch over us, that we may never do bad." Yes, Jesus wants all of us to rise from our graves to live forever with Him in heaven.

Liturgical

He wants that so much that He gave us Holy Communion to help us. When Jesus comes into our heart, He gets our soul ready for heaven. Yes, He does even more. He makes our body, too, ready for heaven. We will say this prayer often: "Dear Jesus, come very soon into my heart. Make my body pure for You. Make it ready for heaven. Come, Lord Jesus, come!"

Posters: motto lettering. Suggestions: "Jesus, help us to be good." "Come, Lord Jesus, come!" *Activity*

The external decorum befitting a proper welcome to our Lord in Holy Communion might be mentioned *Religious Practice* and shown here: cleanliness of the body and clothes, proper folding of the hands, reverent walking to and from the Communion rail, etc.

The lessons on the fundamental points of all virtue, *Remarks* namely, love of God and love of our neighbor for the sake of God, are followed by these two lessons on the reward of virtue, the immortality of the soul and the resurrection of the body. This is the natural sequence. You will notice that in these two latter instructions the positive side of divine revelation has been adhered to strictly. No arguments from reason were advanced, and no speculative development of the teaching was given.

The reason for telling the Gospel stories of how Jesus raised the dead to life will be quite apparent. What better proof could one offer little children for the resurrection of the body, what better appeal to their faith, than the stories of how He, Who proclaimed this future resurrection, showed Himself the Lord of death and resurrection by actually bringing the dead back to life?

Part Five

FRIENDS AND ENEMIES OF JESUS' TEACHING

Pictures

Devices
Jesus Chooses His Apostles
A Missionary of Today Preaching to the Pagans

Introduction

Procedure Jesus taught the people many beautiful and happy lessons. He told them that they had to love God and their neighbor. How many big commandments did He give them? What is the first and greatest commandment? What is the commandment that is like the first? Now Jesus promised a great reward for those who keep these commandments. He promised to take their soul to heaven and at the end of the world to take their body, too, with Him to heaven. But those who do not keep these commandments, He said, would be punished. God will cast their body and soul into hell.

Many people heard Jesus say these things. To-day, I want to tell you about two kinds of people who heard Jesus.

Presentation

The good people followed Jesus in great crowds to hear His teaching and to receive good things from Him. They believed His words. From among those who believed in Him, Jesus picked out certain ones as His special friends and helpers. These are called the disciples of Jesus.

Later, Jesus picked out twelve men from these disciples. (*Show the picture.*) These twelve men were always with Him. They heard everything He said. They saw everything He did. They learned all that He said and did, so that when Jesus would no longer be on earth they could preach and correctly instruct the people about Him, the Savior of the world (Luke 6, 12 ff.). These twelve disciples are called the Apostles of Jesus.

Then Jesus also had seventy-two disciples as His special helpers. He sent them out, two and two, to those places where He planned to go. Besides the disciples and Apostles, there were many other good men and pious women who also believed in the holy teaching of Jesus. They liked to follow Jesus and listen to His words.

But the bad people, those that wanted to stay bad, did not like to hear the Savior's words. It made them angry when He pointed out their sins and told them to do better. They hated Jesus. The good people were happy when they listened to Jesus; but the bad people were very, very angry. The good people were in wonder when they heard His beautiful words of truth, but the bad people were very much troubled (Mark 1, 22). When the good people saw the great wonders of Jesus, they cried out: "No one can do the things You do, unless God is with him" (John 3, 2). But the bad people said: "Jesus does these things with the help of the devil" (Luke 11, 15).

Recapitulation

Now tell me, dear children, what you have just heard about the good Jesus. When He preached such holy words, did many persons come to hear Him? What else did the Savior do besides teach-

ing, when the sick, the blind, and the deaf came to
Him? Do you still remember how many people
were with Jesus that day He fed them all with five
loaves of bread? Did all the people believe the
words of Jesus? Which ones only? Whom did Jesus
pick out from among those who believed in Him?
What name do you give to those who promised
Jesus to do whatever He commanded them? Jesus
then picked out twelve men from among these disciples. What do you call these twelve men? What
work did the Savior want the twelve Apostles to
do? How many more did Jesus pick out from among
those who believed in Him? Were there any other
people, besides the Apostles and the disciples, who
followed Jesus? Did the bad people, too, believe in
Jesus? Did they love Him?

Oral Completion Test

1. The good people were glad when they heard
Jesus, but the bad people were . . .

2. The good people were in wonder at Jesus'
teaching, but the bad people were . . .

3. The good people said He was sent by God,
but the bad people said He did everything with the
help of the . . .

1. Children, we will believe Jesus. We will be- *Application*
lieve that He is the Son of God. We will be good.

We will live as He told us. We will be His little
friends. If we do this, then God the Father in heav-
en will love us.

2. Now children, I have a little story for you
about a girl called Theresa.[4] One day Theresa was
sitting with many other little girls in a large hall.
They were waiting anxiously for a great missionary,
who was coming to tell them how to love Jesus and
how to get other people to love Him, too. (*Show
the picture.*) After a short while the missionary
came.

The good priest told them stories and showed
them pictures of his work among the black people of
Africa. (*A few pictures illustrating the labors of
missionaries might be shown here.*) Then Father
pointed out three ways that they could help get
other people to love Jesus. First of all comes prayer.
This is the prayer he taught them:

> Infant Jesus, help us and
> help the poor heathen children.

"In the second place," he said, "you can offer up your
Holy Communion once a week for some poor sinners.
You can go to Holy Communion in their place to get

---

[4]Adapted from *Ten Eager Hearts*, by a Sister of Notre
Dame (London: Sands & Co.; St. Louis: B. Herder Book
Company, 1924), p. 42.

God's help for them. Lastly, you can put some of the pennies and nickels that your Daddy gives you for candy and shows into the mission bank to buy food and clothes for the poor heathen children."

Two weeks later was Theresa's First Communion Day. This is the little prayer she whispered to Jesus hidden in her heart. "Dear Jesus, this Communion is for me. I want You to give me many, many graces; but tomorrow I am coming for Daddy and Mamma. You know, dear Jesus, that they do not love You as they should. They never go to church; they never take You into their hearts. So I am coming in their place to get graces for them."

Next morning early, Theresa crept out of her little bed, slipped on her clothes, and went quietly down the stairs. She closed the front door very gently and then hurried down the street to the church. There she received her Jesus as she had promised. She prayed very hard that Daddy and Mother would soon come to love Jesus as they should. She hurried home quickly, tiptoed upstairs and slipped back into bed before either her father or mother were awake.

The next morning the little girl did the same, and the next, and the next, until she had been to Communion six or seven times. But the last time, her Daddy was awake and looked out of the window just in time to see his little girl hurrying down the street. When Theresa returned, her father met her at the door.

"Where have you been?" he asked.

"Oh, Daddy, don't be angry," cried Theresa. "I did not want to go to heaven without you, and each morning I have been to Jesus to get graces for you and Mamma, that you might go to heaven, too."

Just then Mother came downstairs. The whole story was repeated to her. What could Father and Mother say to these loving words of their darling child? Their hearts were touched.

"Go on praying for us," they said, "and we will come too."

The next time Theresa went to Holy Communion, Daddy and Mamma went along. She, a little girl of seven, had been Jesus' little missionary — she had taught her parents to love the Savior. Children, would you not like to teach someone to love Him too?

Prayer

Infant Jesus, help us and help the poor heathen children.

Religious Practice

The time allotted to the culminating activity might be used in this unit to help the little ones make their examination of conscience. No set form, commonly called Table of Sins, should be given to beginners. However, the flash cards or blackboard summaries containing the substance of the ten commandments (found in Parts One and Two of this unit) should be used as a basis for the examination of conscience. The teacher could ask categorical questions about each one of these. The answers are to be made in the confessional. For example: GOD WANTS US TO PRAY—Did you miss your daily prayers? GOD WANTS US TO SPEAK HIS NAME WITH LOVE—Did you speak His name in anger or in fun? GOD WANTS US TO GO TO MASS ON SUNDAY — Did you stay away from Mass on Sunday through your own fault? GOD WANTS US NOT TO EAT MEAT ON FRIDAY — Did you eat meat on Friday when you knew it was Friday? GOD WANTS US TO BE KIND AND OBEDIENT TO OUR PARENTS — Did you disobey your parents or answer them back? GOD WANTS US TO BE KIND TO ALL PEOPLE — Did you quarrel or fight with other people? GOD WANTS US TO KEEP OUR SOUL AND BODY PURE — Did you look at impure things? touch yourself impurely? or others? or let others touch you? GOD WANTS US TO BE HONEST WITH ALL PEOPLE — Did you take something that did not belong to you? What was it? GOD WANTS US TO TELL THE TRUTH TO ALL PEOPLE — Did you tell a lie?

The children should be impressed with the neces-

sity of answering these questions in their own minds
truthfully. Tell them to answer truthfully any question the priest asks them. In the confessional the
little ones tell in their own way the sins they have
found through your questioning. It is a good idea
to tell them that if there is anything they do not
know how to say they should tell the priest: Father,
there is something I do not know how to say;
please help me.

UNIT EIGHT

Content

1. Jesus Will Soon Die.
2. Holy Thursday.
3. Jesus Suffers for Us.
4. Jesus Dies and is Buried.

Objectives

1. To know one of the fundamental doctrines of Catholic Faith: man's redemption through the passion and death of Jesus.

2. To acquire a hatred of our sins that made Jesus suffer so much.

3. To inflame our hearts with love toward Jesus; to love Him for what He has suffered for us.

Part One

JESUS WILL SOON DIE

Pictures

Triumphal Entry of Jesus into Jerusalem
(Schumacher)

A Procession in Honor of the Holy Eucharist

Devices

Introduction

You still remember how Jesus went with His
parents to Jerusalem for the great feast when He
was twelve years old. All the people who were old
enough had to visit the church at Jerusalem on this
feast day. Today I am going to tell you what happened when Jesus made His last visit to Jerusalem.

Procedure

Presentation

1. Jesus did not live long on this earth. He was
thirty years old when He began to teach, and He
taught only three years. Now in the last year of
Jesus' life here on earth, He took His twelve Apostles with Him to Jerusalem to celebrate the great
feast for the last time. On the way Jesus said to
His Apostles: "See, we are going to Jerusalem, and
there everything shall happen to the Savior of the

177

world, as God foretold long ago through holy men. The Savior shall be mocked and made fun of, scourged with whips, and spit upon. After they have scourged Him, they shall put Him to death. But He shall rise again from the grave on the third day" (Luke 18, 31 ff.).

See! Jesus knew before time what He was going to suffer for us. He even told His Apostles beforehand. But these good Apostles loved the dear Jesus so much, that they wanted to have Him always with them. It was too hard to think that Jesus would be scourged, made fun of, spit upon, and killed. They did not understand it. Jesus' words were hidden from them. They did not catch the meaning of what He said (Luke 18, 34).

2. Jesus was making His last journey to Jerusalem. When He came near to the city, a great crowd of good people who believed in Him marched along with Him. (*Show the picture.*) They carried branches of trees in their hands and as they went along they cried out with joy: "Blessed is He Who comes in the name of the Lord" (Matt. 21, 8, 9). That was seven days before the great feast.

3. The bad people in Jerusalem were very angry that Jesus received such a celebration when He came into their city. The leaders of these bad people met together and planned to kill Jesus.

During the next few days, Jesus taught the great crowds of people that came to hear Him. (Matt. chaps. 21–25; Mark chaps. 11–13; Luke chaps. 19–21.) He spoke hard words to the bad people and scolded them for their sins. He told them the punishment of God would surely come upon them. At night Jesus did not stay in the city. He left when it grew dark and came back the next morning to teach again.

Recapitulation

1. Tell me, children, what you have just learned. Did Jesus live long on earth? How many years did Jesus live on earth? How many years did He teach? When the day of the great feast came in the last year of His life on earth, where did He go? Whom did He take with Him? He told the Apostles that something would happen to Him there. What was it Jesus told them? Did the Apostles understand what He meant?

2. What happened when Jesus came near to the city of Jerusalem? What did the good people do? What did they say about Jesus? How many days before the great feast did this happen?

3. What did the bad people do when they heard about the great celebration Jesus had when He came to their city? What did their leaders plan to

do? What did Jesus do the next few days after He came to Jerusalem. Did He teach only the good people? What other kind of people did He teach? What did He tell these bad people would happen to them? Did Jesus stay in their city overnight? Where did He go? Children, in our next lesson we will learn what happened to Jesus during the next few days.

Doctrinal

Application

Children, to whom did God first promise the Savior? Why did Adam and Eve need a Savior? Yes, they were disobedient to God; they sinned. They deserved God's punishment. If God had not been kind and sent them the Savior, they would have been unhappy forever. But that is not all. We, too, became bad through the sin of the first man and woman. If the Savior had not come, we should be unhappy forever. But the Savior saved us from God's punishment. He did this by suffering in our place. Tell me some things that Jesus told the Apostles He was going to suffer.

O children! See how much Jesus loved us! He wanted to suffer for us. He wanted to suffer so much and so hard, that God would forgive us that never-ending punishment for our sins. Let us love the dear Jesus. Let us please Him by living as He told us to. Let us try to live as He lived.

Liturgical — Palm Sunday, Processions

1. Children, every year on the Sunday before Easter we think of the story of Jesus entering Jerusalem. On that day, palms are brought into the church. Prayers are said over them and they are blessed. (*Show a palm branch.*) We call this day Palm Sunday. After the palms are blessed, the priest and the mass servers, carrying a piece of the blessed palm in their hand, march to the rear of the church. The choir then sings a song in praise of Jesus. When the song is finished, the mass servers and the priest march solemnly back into the church and up to the altar.

When this takes place on Palm Sunday this year, of what things that happened long ago will you think? In whose honor is the procession of palms held? What do we think of in the life of Jesus?

2. Children, did you ever hear of any other procession that is held in church in honor of Jesus? Were you ever in church when the little boys and girls and the mass servers marched through the church, with the priest coming at the end, carrying the monstrance? (*Show a picture of the monstrance.*)

Who is in the monstrance? Yes, Jesus. The priest has taken Him out of His little house on the altar and has put Him into the center of the monstrance. Perhaps you have seen how the little mass servers carry candles in their hands and how the little girls, all dressed in white, tear up their flowers and drop them on the floor of the church. All this is done for Jesus. And did you see how the people bow their heads when Jesus in the monstrance passes by? These people are bowing their heads because Jesus is God. They are saying a little prayer, asking Jesus to bless them and help them. You should do the same.

Bowing the Head

Religious Practice Teach the children to bow their heads properly and reverently. Train the little ones to avoid bury· ing their heads hurriedly, as is so often done by their elders.

Double Genuflection

Some time ago, children, we learned how to genu flect when we come into church. (*Have one of the children demonstrate.*) Today, I want to show you how to make a genuflection on two knees. First. you kneel down on both knees and then you bow your head, just as you learned to do a few minutes ago. As soon as you have bowed your head, you rise from your knees. (*Have one or two of the children demonstrate how it is done, then practice together.*) Children, this is called the double genuflection. You should make the double genuflection whenever Jesus is in the monstrance on the altar. You make the double genuflection then instead of the single genuflection.

Have the children join in a little procession around the classroom. The reverent gait, the casting down of the eyes, the folding of the hands, can be practiced here in preparation for their use in approaching and leaving the Communion rail. *Activity*

Sing a simple hymn in honor of Jesus in the Holy Eucharist.[1] *Hymn*

Part Two

HOLY THURSDAY

Pictures

The Last Supper (Schumacher)
The Agony in the Garden (Schumacher)
Jesus Taken Prisoner (Schumacher) *Devices*

---

[1] *Diocesan Hymnal I,* by Most Reverend Joseph Schrembs, D.D. (New York: J. Fischer & Bros., 1928).

Introduction

Children, even among the Apostles of our dear Lord Jesus there was one who was very bad. His name was Judas. I am going to tell you today what Judas did to Jesus.

Presentation

1. Judas liked money so much that he did not mind doing anything bad if he was paid for it. He knew that the leaders of the Jews wanted to kill Jesus. He knew, too, that they wanted to get hold of Jesus on the quiet, so that the people would not see them. So on the Wednesday after Jesus entered Jerusalem in so much glory, Judas went to the Jewish leaders and said to them: "What will you give me if I show you where you can take Jesus on the quiet?" They promised Judas thirty pieces of silver, which is about twenty dollars in our money. The wicked Apostle then agreed to come at the right time and turn Jesus over to His enemies. The Jewish leaders were glad and they made up their minds that Jesus must die.

O unhappy Judas! How wickedly he acts against Jesus, His Master!

All this happened during the week when the Jews were supposed to kill and eat a lamb.

2. On Thursday evening Jesus gathered His twelve Apostles together in a house to eat this lamb with them. (*Show the picture.*) While they were at table, Jesus took bread in His hands, blessed it, and said: "This is My Body." Then He gave It to His Apostles to eat: It loked like bread, but it was the TRUE BODY OF JESUS they were eating. Jesus said so and the Apostles believed it. The living Jesus came into their hearts. That was the First Holy Communion of the Apostles. Afterwards Jesus took a cup of wine, blessed it, and said: "This is My Blood." Then He gave it to His Apostles to drink. They received Jesus' true Body and Blood.

3. Afterwards Jesus began to be sad. Speaking to His Apostles, He said: "One of you is going to hand Me over to My enemies. I am going. But woe to that man who will betray Me. It would be better for him, if he had never been born." The Apostles were frightened. Some of them began to ask: "Lord, am I the one?" Even Judas asked: "Lord, am I the one?" And Jesus whispered to him: "Yes, you are the one."

Soon after, Judas arose and went out. Jesus stayed at the table with the other Apostles. He told them that He was soon going away, back to His Father. The Apostles were sad when they heard this. But Jesus tried to make them happy by telling them that there were many nice places in His Father's house. He would come back again, He said, to take them with Him to His Father. He promised, too, to send them the Holy Ghost. He told them to love one another and to hold firmly to His teachings. He prayed to His Father for them and for all of us who would believe in Him.

Then Jesus, with His Apostles, went outside of the city as He had done on the other nights. He walked up the Mount of Olives to a farm in which there was a garden. There were many olive trees in this garden. So it was called the Garden of Olives. On the way, Jesus said to His Apostles: "This very night you shall all leave Me." But Peter excitedly spoke up: "Even though all leave You, I will not do so." Then Jesus said to Peter: "Yes, before the rooster crows twice this night, you will say three times that you are not My disciple." Still Peter would not listen. "Even though I must die with You," he cried out, "I will not deny You." The other Apostles agreed with Peter.

You remember, children, that Judas had left before. He knew that Jesus was going to spend the night on the Mount of Olives. So he went to the Jewish leaders and asked them for soldiers. He would lead them to the place where they could take Jesus prisoner.

4. When Jesus came to the farm on the Mount of Olives, He left eight of His disciples behind. He took only three of them with Him into the garden: Peter, James, and John. Jesus wanted to pray with them to His heavenly Father. Then Jesus began to be afraid. The things He was soon going to suffer made Him afraid. I have told you already that Jesus would be mocked, scourged with whips, and be put to death to save us from our sins. The picture of all these terrible, cruel sufferings passed before the Savior's eyes. The many, many sins of all the people were heavy and they pressed down on Jesus' heart. These sins were very hateful to God. That hurt the Heart of Jesus. It hurt Him, too, to think that so many people would die without being sorry for their sins. These people would lose their souls, and Jesus wanted to make them all so happy.

Then Jesus said to the three Apostles: "I am very, very sad. Wait here and watch with Me." (*Show the picture.*) Then He went on a little farther, fell upon His knees, then upon His face. From His lips there came this prayer: "Father! Good Father! If it is possible, do not let Me suffer; still, let it be done, not as I want, but as You want." Three times Jesus said this same prayer. His fears began to grow. He was soon to start His painful sufferings. He was going to do penance for many great sins. Yes, He was going to suffer; but for many people His sufferings would do no good, because they would continue to lead bad lives. These thoughts made His fears so great, that He began to sweat. He did not sweat drops of water, as we do when we are afraid; but drops of blood that fell from His holy face to the ground.

At last Jesus finished His prayer with these words: "If this suffering cannot be taken from Me, may God's Will be done." His heavenly Father then sent an angel who made Jesus strong to suffer everything.

With these heart pains, Jesus begins His sufferings for us. How terrible sin is that Jesus must suffer such pains!

As Jesus finished His prayer, the soldiers sent by the Jewish leaders came into the garden with their lanterns, spears, and clubs. Judas was with them. He had told the soldiers: "The one I kiss is Jesus. Take hold of Him, and be careful that He does not get away." Jesus came forward to meet the soldiers. His Apostles followed behind Him. The dear Savior said to the soldiers: "For whom are you looking?" They cried out: "Jesus of Nazareth." "I am Jesus of Nazareth," the Savior answered. The soldiers were very much frightened and fell to the ground. When they stood up again, Jesus asked them the same question: "For whom are you looking?" And when they said, "Jesus of Nazareth," He told them again: "I said before that I am Jesus of Nazareth. If you are looking for Me, then let these Apostles go free." Just then Judas stepped forward. (*Show the picture.*) He put his arms about the Savior's neck and said: "Greetings, dear Master." Then he kissed Jesus. Wicked Judas! But still Jesus spoke kindly to him: "Judas, what did you come for? With a kiss you betray Me to My enemies."

The soldiers now crowded around Jesus. The Savior, without moving, let them tie His hands, and lead Him as a prisoner out of the garden. He was then hurried to the city, where the Jewish leaders were anxiously waiting for Him. The Apostles, just as Jesus had said, all ran away.

Children, your hearts must be beating fast as you listen to this story. O unhappy Judas! He kissed the Savior to betray Him into the hands of His enemies. That kiss was a sign to the soldiers that this was Jesus. And oh! the dear, good Savior! How kindly and softly He speaks to unhappy and ungrateful Judas!

Recapitulation

1. Children! I am sad when I think of the things I have just told you. The dear Jesus! Unhappy

Judas! What did Judas do on Wednesday? What did he tell the Jewish leaders? How much money did they promise him for this? And Judas loved the miserable money so much that he promised to hand Jesus over to His enemies. Wasn't that terrible? He had lived with Jesus, his Master, for three years. He had heard so many holy words from His lips. He had so often seen the kind deeds and the great wonders of that Savior. Hateful, hateful sin!

2. What did Jesus do on Thursday? What did the Jews have to do during that week? And what did Jesus also do on Thursday evening? What did Jesus give His Apostles to eat besides the lamb? What words did Jesus speak over the bread? What words over the wine? After Jesus spoke these words over the bread and wine, what did they then become? The Apostles received the Body and Blood of Jesus into their hearts. They received Holy Communion.

3. Judas was at the Last Supper. Who knew what Judas was planning in his heart? What did Jesus say to His Apostles? See how the dear Jesus warned Judas so kindly against his terrible plan! And when Judas boldly asked, "Lord, am I the one?" Jesus still spoke kindly to him. The heart of Judas was hard. He could no longer stay in the room with Jesus and the other Apostles, so he went out into the darkness of the night. How did Jesus

know what Judas was planning? Yes, the Son of God knows all things.

What else did the Savior say to His Apostles? How did He comfort them? What did He promise them? What did He tell them to do? He prayed for them, too. What did He pray for? For whom else did He pray? Children, we will believe firmly in Jesus and in His teachings. We will love God and be obedient to Him. That will please Him. Then we can hope that Jesus will take us, too, to Himself in the house of His heavenly Father, just as He promised the Apostles.

Where did Jesus go then with His disciples? What did He tell them they would do that very night? What did Peter answer? What did Jesus say to Peter? And how did Peter answer this? What did the other Apostles tell Jesus? But we shall see later on that the Apostles, even Peter, did just what Jesus said they would. Jesus, the Son of God, knows all things.

4. What did Jesus do when He came to the farm on the Mount of Olives? How many disciples did He take with Him into the garden? Did He stay with these three? What did He do when He was all alone? See how devoutly Jesus prays to His heavenly Father! How should you pray? Jesus knelt down. So when you pray, you should kneel down.

Jesus kept His thoughts on His heavenly Father and spoke devoutly to Him. So when you pray, you should keep your thoughts on God and speak devoutly to Him.

Jesus knew all things. He knew all the things He was going to suffer. What did He feel in His heart when He thought of His sufferings? When He thought that He was going to do all that as punishment for the sins of all men, did His heart hurt still more? Yes, His fear, too, became so great that He began to sweat. What did Jesus sweat?

Application   1. Children, every Thursday evening we ought to think of Jesus' suffering in the Garden of Olives. Especially on the Thursday before Easter we ought to think of these sufferings. This Thursday we call Holy Thursday.

Now let us thank Jesus that He suffered so much in His Heart for us. Thanks, dear Jesus, for all You suffered for us! (*Have the children repeat this two or three times.*) Our sins made You suffer so much. We hate our sins. We are sorry for them and we will not do them again.

(*The teacher should have the children call to mind their sins against the first three commandments. After each commandment, have them say the following little act of sorrow together.*) "Jesus, my sins made You suffer. I hate them because they made You suffer. Jesus, take my sins away. I do not want them any more."

2. Children, never act like Judas. Poor Judas! He should have been sorry and stopped sinning. But what did he do? Yes, he kept on sinning. His heart became hard. Never let your heart grow hard in sin.

3. We heard before what Jesus did with the bread and wine on Holy Thursday. Can you tell me what He did? Children, the priest does the same thing in every holy Mass. Jesus told the priest to do this. At Mass the priest takes the host in his hands, just as Jesus took the bread into His holy hands at the Last Supper. Then the priest says the very same words Jesus said that night: This is My Body. At that moment Jesus comes on the altar. The host is changed into Jesus. In the same way, the priest says the words of the dear Savior over the wine in the chalice: This is My Blood. At that very moment the wine is changed into Jesus. When you are at Mass, remember that the same thing happens on the altar that Jesus did at the Last Supper.

Little penances for Jesus: Kneeling very straight at Mass; being very quiet and attentive in school. *Religious Practice* Link up with "Our Preparation for Holy Communion."

Part Three

JESUS SUFFERS FOR US

Pictures

The Scourging (Schumacher)

Devices   The Crowning With Thorns (Schumacher)

Ecce Homo

Jesus Carries His Cross (Schumacher)

Introduction

In our last lesson, children, we saw how Judas
Procedure sold Jesus for thirty pieces of silver. We saw, too,
how Jesus let the soldiers tie His hands and take
Him prisoner out of the Garden of Olives. Now you
want to hear what happened to the Savior, don't
you? Listen carefully.

Presentation

1. The soldiers took the dear Jesus to the house
of the Jewish high priest. The leaders of the Jews
were all there, too. They asked Jesus all kinds of
questions and accused Him of all kinds of bad
teaching and preaching. But they could not find
Him guilty, because He had never said nor done
anything bad. At last the high priest asked Jesus
this question: "Are You the Son of God?" (Matt.

26, 63–67.) Jesus answered truly: "Yes, I am, and you shall some day see Me coming with power and glory in the clouds of heaven." The high priest did not like to believe that Jesus was the Son of God. So he cried out: "He is mocking God! He deserves to die for that!" The leaders all chimed in: "Yes, He deserves to die!"

Then they led Jesus to prison. And Judas got his thirty pieces of silver.

While Jesus was inside the house of the high priest, two of His Apostles, Peter and John, stayed in the yard outside. They loved their Master and they wanted to see what was going to happen to Him (Matt. 26; Mark 14; John 18). Outside in the yard, the soldiers who had taken Jesus prisoner stood in a group. They had built a fire and were standing around it to warm themselves. Peter came up and joined the soldiers. Just then a servant girl passed by. She looked at Peter and said: "You are also a disciple of Jesus, aren't you?" Peter answered right back: "Woman, I do not even know Him!" Just then the rooster crowed. Peter started to walk away from the crowd. But another servant girl saw him and said to him: "Yes, sure you are one of His disciples." Again Peter said "No." Then those who were standing about spoke together: "You certainly are one of His disciples." Then Peter began to curse and swear. A third time he said that he did not even know Jesus. The rooster crowed a second time. Children, do you still remember what Jesus told Peter? "Before the rooster crows twice this night, you will say three times that you are not My disciple."

Just then the soldiers marched through the yard with Jesus. They were taking Him to prison. Jesus passed by Peter. The dear Savior looked sadly at Peter (Luke 22, 61–62). At once poor Peter thought of what Jesus had told him that evening. He went out of the yard and began to cry bitter tears. Poor Peter! Good Peter! He had sinned. But quickly, very quickly he was sorry and sinned no more.

The next few hours Jesus was kept in prison. These were hard hours for the Savior. The soldiers made fun of Him. They spit on Him. They blindfolded Him and hit Him in the face. Then they laughed at Him and said: "Tell us now who hit You?" Jesus knew, but He suffered everything without a word. He did not answer back even once. Do you remember, children, that Jesus told the Apostles beforehand that the people would spit on Him and make fun of Him? So it happened.

2. Early Friday morning the Jewish leaders came together in the high priest's house. Once again they

said: Jesus must die. Then they took our dear Savior to the Roman Governor, whose name was Pontius Pilate. They wanted Pilate to condemn Jesus to death.

When poor Judas saw them taking Jesus to Pilate to be condemned to death, he became frightened. He was sorry he had betrayed Jesus, his Master. He could not bear to keep the money, the thirty pieces of silver, any longer. He carried it to the high priests. "I have sinned," he cried. "I have betrayed a just and innocent man!" But the high priests only laughed at him. "What difference does that make to us?" they asked. Then Judas threw the money down on the floor. He ran out of the room, got a rope, and hanged himself from a tree (Matt. 27, 3–5). Children, see what happens to a hardened sinner. What a terrible end! Be careful not to sin! Sin easily leads to a sad end.

The Jewish leaders then accused the Holy Lord Jesus before the Governor, Pontius Pilate. They wanted Jesus to be condemned to death right away. "He mocked God," they said, "because He told us He is the Son of God. He is a bad leader of the people, because He said He is the King of Jews, and the Jews have only one King, the Emperor at Rome."

Pilate asked about the things the Jewish leaders

said against Jesus. But he could find nothing bad
in Jesus. Then the Jewish leaders whispered to the
people to shout out, "Crucify Him! Crucify Him!"
(John, chaps. 18–19.) Pilate knew that our dear
Jesus was altogether innocent. So he said to the
noisy crowd: "I find no fault in Him. But this is
the great feast day, and I usually free a prisoner
for you on this day. Choose now between two. Shall
I leave Jesus go free or Barabbas who is a very
bad man and a murderer?" A shout went up from
the crowd: "Not Jesus, but free Barabbas!"

After this, Pilate ordered Jesus to be scourged
with whips. The dear Jesus was tied to a pillar, and
whipped and whipped until His skin and flesh were
cut open. (*Show the picture.*)

Pilate then let the soldiers make fun of Jesus in a
very cruel and painful way. Jesus had said that He
was a King. A King, as you know, wears a purple
cloak, he has a crown on his head, and holds in his
hand a golden stick, which we call a scepter. In fun,
the soldiers put a red rag about Jesus' shoulders.
(*Show the picture.*) They placed a crown of thorns
on His head. And into His hand they pushed a little,
broken stick. They knelt down before Jesus in fun.
They spit at Him and hit Him on the cheek. With
heavy clubs they hit the crown of thorns on His
head — and oh! the points of the thorns pierced

into His head. These cruel soldiers mocked Jesus
and said: "Hail! King of the Jews!" And they hit
Him again and again in the face.

Poor Jesus! Dear Jesus! He suffered everything
like a lamb, without a word. Oh! how many hurts
and pains Jesus suffered for our sins!

After the scourging and crowning with thorns,
Pilate took Jesus and showed Him to the people.
"Look at the Man!" he said. (*Show the picture.*)
But the Jews shouted: "Away with Him! Away
with Him! Crucify Him!" Pilate then called for
a basin of water. He washed his hands and said:
"Take Him and crucify Him, but I do not want to
take the blame for the Blood of this innocent Man"
(Matt. 27, 24–25). The Jews were wild. "May His
Blood come upon us and upon our children!" they
shouted. That means: "If the killing of Jesus deserves to be punished by God, let that punishment
come upon us and upon our children and upon our
children's children forever."

Pilate now turned Jesus over to His enemies. They
could crucify Him right away. Children, crucifixion
was a very cruel death. First of all, the one to be
crucified had to carry his own cross, which was very
heavy, to the place of crucifixion. Then he was
nailed to the cross by his hands and feet. He had to
hang there on the cross until he died in pain; or

if he lived too long, the bones of his hands and legs were broken with clubs.

So they placed the heavy cross on Jesus' shoulders. The Savior had to go along with two bad men who were condemned to death for great crimes. The crucifixion was to take place outside the city on a hill called Calvary. Poor Jesus! He had to suffer so much on Thursday night and Friday morning that He could not even carry the cross alone. So the Jews forced a stranger to help Him carry it. (*Show picture*)

When they came to Calvary, they crucified Jesus and the two thieves, putting Jesus in the middle. It was about ten o'clock Friday morning when they crucified Jesus. I shall tell you more about this in our next lesson.

Recapitulation

1. Children, where did the soldiers take Jesus from the garden? What did they do to Jesus when they had Him before the high priest? Could they prove anything bad against Him? What question did the high priest finally ask Him? What did the Savior answer? What He said was true. He said that He was the Son of God and that His enemies would one day see Him coming in the clouds of heaven. But the wicked high priest would not be-

lieve Jesus. What did he think of Jesus' answer? What did he cry out? What did the others shout? Where did they take Jesus then?

While Jesus was in the house of the high priest, what happened in the yard outside? Who was out in the yard? What were these soldiers doing? What was Peter doing? What did the servant girl say to Peter? How did Peter answer? How many times did he say that he did not know Jesus? What reminded Peter of what the Savior had told him? When the soldiers marched through the yard with Jesus, whom did they meet? Then Peter remembered what Jesus had said. What did he do then?

2. Children, it hurts me too much to tell you any more just now of the story of Jesus' sufferings. I know it hurts you too. But let me see if you remember what Jesus suffered Friday morning. What did the Jewish leaders do early Friday morning? What did they say must be done to Jesus? Where did they take Him then? What was the governor's name?

While Jesus was before Pilate, what was poor, wicked Judas doing? Was he glad now that he had turned Jesus over to His enemies? Was he happy with the thirty pieces of silver that he got for his great sin? How did he feel about what he had done? He told the Jewish leaders that he had done something very bad and hateful to God. He would have been glad if Jesus had made Himself free. Jesus could have made Himself free, but He wanted to die for us and for our sins.

But, children, Judas was not really sorry. He would have been glad if Jesus had freed Himself and if He did not have to die. *But Judas did not turn back to Jesus, as Peter did.* Judas did not feel bad about his wicked deed like Peter did about his sin. Peter was very, very sorry that he had denied his Master three times.

Where did Judas go after he saw the Jews taking Jesus to Pilate? What did he say to the high priests? And what did they do? What did they say to Him? Children, never do anything bad to please bad people. Even if you are later sorry that you did bad, the bad people will only laugh at you for helping them. What did Judas do with the thirty pieces of silver he got for his great sin? What did he do after he left the room? Terrible! Bad Judas! Poor Judas! He ends all with the worst thing he could do. He forgets God's love, and is lost forever. Children, this hardened sinner had a bad end, a very bad end. Listen now to what I tell you! Do not commit sin at all. After one sin, you easily commit a second, a third, a fourth sin; and in the end you will die a sinner and be lost forever.

What happened while Jesus was before Pilate?
What did the Jewish leaders say of the Savior?
What did Jesus call Himself? What did the Jewish
leaders say He deserved for calling Himself the Son
of God? Did Pilate find Jesus guilty? What did he
tell the Jews he would do for them on the great
feast day? What two persons did he put before the
Jews, when he let them pick one to be freed? Who
was Barabbas? What an insult to Jesus! He is put
alongside of Barabbas, a murderer. And the Jews
cried out that Pilate should free Barabbas. What
did Pilate let the soldiers do to Jesus then? Oh!
what terrible pains Jesus suffered for sin — for our
sins, too! Let us not sin again! What did the soldiers do to Jesus after the scourging? How did they
insult and hurt Him? What did they put on Him
instead of the king's cloak? instead of a golden
crown? in place of a scepter? What did they do
then? And now tell me how Jesus suffered all this.

After Jesus had been scourged and crowned with
thorns, Pilate brought Him before the people. He
thought they would feel sorry for Jesus. But they
did not feel sorry. Instead, what did they cry out?
What did Pilate do then? Pilate was a bad judge,
wasn't he? He found no fault in Jesus, but still he
let the Savior be crucified. Before God, Pilate was
guilty of the Blood of Jesus. What did the Jews

say about the Blood of Jesus? Yes, children, the Blood of Jesus comes as punishment upon all who do not believe in Him and who do not live as He teaches. But for us who believe in Him, who love Him, and follow His holy teaching, the Blood of Jesus brings us heaven and happiness forever.

Where did they take Jesus after Pilate sentenced Him to death? Did Jesus have to carry the cross? When Jesus became too weak to carry the cross alone, what did the Jews do? On Mount Calvary they nailed Jesus to the cross. Who was crucified alongside of Jesus? Just as if Jesus were the greatest sinner! Yes, it was for the sins of all men that Jesus was suffering such terrible pains. Jesus is innocent, too. He is holy. He is the Son of God.

Application Children, often think of these sufferings of Jesus. Think of them whenever you look at a crucifix. Say to yourself: Jesus suffered all that for my sins. I will not make Him suffer any more, I will stay away from sin, I will stay away from bad people who lead me to sin.

(*The teacher should have the children call to mind their sins against the last seven commandments. After each commandment, have them look at a large crucifix and say the following little act of sorrow together.*) "Jesus, my sins made You suffer like that. I hate them because they made You suffer. Jesus, take my sins away. I do not want them any more."

Night Prayers — emphasizing Contrition as a *Prayer* part of these prayers.

Little penances for Jesus: Giving up candy. Link up with "Our Preparation for Holy Communion." *Religious Practice*

The "penance" the priest gives us in confession — a little punishment for our sins.

Part Four

JESUS DIES AND IS BURIED

Pictures

The Crucifixion Group (Schumacher)
The Burial of Jesus   *Devices*

Introduction

Who will tell us what the soldiers did to Jesus after they had whipped Him? Then when they had *Procedure* crowned Him with thorns, Pilate showed Him to the people. Pilate thought the people might feel sorry when they saw poor Jesus suffering so much. But they did not feel sorry. What did they want to do to Jesus? What did they cry out with a loud voice?

Presentation

1. Yes, that is just what they did to poor Jesus; they nailed Him to the cross. (*Show the picture.*) Just think! Jesus hung upon the cross until three o'clock in the afternoon. His sufferings all that time were very, very great. The Jewish leaders stood near the cross and made fun of Jesus. "He helped others," they said, "but He cannot help Himself. If He is the Savior, let Him come down from the cross and we will believe in Him. If God loves Him, then let God free Him, for He said that He is the Son of God." Now listen, children, to how Jesus answered all this. Looking up to heaven, He said to His Father: "Forgive them, for they do not know what they are doing." Children! Jesus prays to His Father for these cruel, wicked men. He asks His Father not to punish them, but to forgive them these terrible sins.

Holy Mother Mary, the dear Apostle John, and some pious women were also standing near the cross. They had been there when Jesus was nailed to the cross. They were sad, so sad that their hearts felt like bursting, when they saw how the Savior was suffering. Mary, the holy Mother, and John, the Apostle whom Jesus loved, stood there at the feet

of the Savior all the while He hung on the cross.
Once Jesus looked down on them and spoke some
golden words. To Mary He said: "Mother! John
is now your son." And to the Apostle John He
said: "She is now your Mother." From that time
on, the dear Apostle John took care of holy Mary
as a good son takes care of his dear mother.

At twelve o'clock noon darkness came over the
earth. The sun did not shine and it remained pitch
dark until three o'clock. Then at three o'clock Jesus
spoke these solemn words: "It is finished! Father,
into Your hands I give My soul!" He bowed His
head. Jesus was dead. The earth trembled and
shook. Rocks split apart. The people were much
afraid and many struck their breasts. The soldier-
captain who stood watch at the foot of the cross
cried out: "Truly, this was the Son of God!"

Prayer. Children, kneel down now and say this
prayer with me. "Jesus, we thank You. You are the
true Son of God. You suffered so many pains for
us. You died such a cruel death on the cross. You
did this, that all our sins might be taken away, that
we might enter heaven and be forever happy with
You there. We thank You. Yes, we will love You
with all our heart. We will obey You and Your
Father in heaven. We will obey You now and al-

ways. We will thank You today and every day until we die. Jesus, help us to keep every word of this promise. Amen."

2. After our good Savior had died, two holy men who secretly believed in Him went to Pontius Pilate. They asked that they might take down Jesus' Body from the cross and bury Him. Pilate called the soldier-captain to find out if Jesus was really dead. One of the soldiers took his long spear and thrust it into Jesus' side. Water and blood came out of the wound — a sign that Jesus was dead. Pilate told the two holy men that they could now take the Body of Jesus. Gently and piously, they took Jesus down from the cross and buried Him in a grave that was carved out of stone. (*Show the picture.*) No one had ever been buried in this grave before. When they had placed the dead Body of Jesus in the grave, they rolled a great stone over the opening. All this took place on Friday afternoon before the going down of the sun. The Jews asked Pilate to have a guard of soldiers watch over the grave of Jesus for three days. They also put a seal on the grave.

Recapitulation

1. Have you remembered this story children? Till what hour did Jesus hang on the cross? What

did the Jews do while He was hanging there? What did they say to make fun of Him? Surely, Jesus could have helped Himself. But He did not want to. Out of love for us He did not want to come down from the cross. He wished to die for love of us. He wished to suffer, so that God might take away our sins and their eternal punishment. He wanted to die to save us. Oh! how we ought to love Him for that! How we ought to thank Him! Yes, even though Jesus suffered so much from those bad people, even though He was made fun of and put to a cruel death by them, still He was not angry at them. How did He pray to His Father for them while He was hanging on the cross?

Who was also there on Mount Calvary with these bad people? Who was standing under the cross of Jesus. How did holy Mary feel? And how did the dear Apostle John feel? Even on the cross, the good Savior wanted to take care of His holy Mother. What did He say to Mary? What did He say to John? What did John do for holy Mary after Jesus was dead? See the dear, good son! How he loves and honors and takes care of his Mother! Children, that is the way you should love and honor your parents. When you grow bigger, work for them and take care of them when they are old. Make their old days happy.

Children, what happened at twelve o'clock noon?
How long did it stay dark? What·words did Jesus
speak at three o'clock? Then He died. What happened when He died? What did the people do when
they felt the earth shake and tremble? What did
the soldier-captain say?

Yes, children, the Son of God saved us by His
sufferings and death on the holy cross. Who created
us? Who saved or redeemed us? Where did the Son
of God save us? What did He do to save us?

2. What did the two holy men do after Jesus'
death? What was done to Jesus' Body that Pilate
knew He was really dead? What came out of the
wound in the side of Jesus? Yes, blood and water
— a sure sign that Jesus was dead. When Pilate
gave the Body of Jesus to the two holy men, where
did they bury Him? What did the Jews do?

1. All this happened on Good Friday. Every
Application Friday we ought to think like this to ourselves: on
this day of the week my dear Jesus suffered and
died for me. We should pray, too, and thank the
Savior that He died to take away our sins. We
should promise Him not to sin again. We should
ask Him to help us stay away from sin.

Do you know what you should especially do
every Friday to show Jesus that you really love
Him? Yes, do not eat meat on Friday. Say to your-

self: Jesus died for me on Friday, so today I will not eat meat out of love for Him. He suffered much for me; I will suffer a little for Him.

2. We should especially pray hard on the Friday before Easter. We call this day Good Friday. On Good Friday we will go to church, even though we do not have to. Oh! how sad everything looks in church. The priest wears black vestments, just like he does at funerals. On Good Friday a large crucifix is placed on the floor of the church near the Communion rail. We should come up to the crucifix, kneel and kiss the hands, feet, and side of Jesus. We ought to do this very devoutly. We should thank the good Savior that He saved us on the cross.

On Good Friday we are very sad. As a sign of our sadness, the bells in the church tower do not ring all day.

(Have the children spread a small cloth and place a little pillow upon which the crucifix can be laid. *Religious* Then have them approach in procession formation *Practice* and have them kneel while they kiss the image of Jesus on the cross.)

Recite together the Act of Contrition (short *Prayer* form).

The teacher will have noticed that the story of Jesus' sufferings is given in rather extensive detail. The rea- *Remarks* sons for this are the following: First, the passion of

Christ is a fundamental doctrine of our faith; second, it contains the story of our redemption through Jesus; third, it shows the heinousness of sin, thereby instilling in the child-heart hatred of sin; fourth, it inflames the hearts of the little ones with the love of God. The teacher has undoubtedly also noticed that many of the minor details in the story of the passion have been omitted, lest the minds of the little children be over-burdened with too much material.

At this point in the instructions, the children are surely well prepared to make their first confession. It is advisable to let the children go to confession at least twice before their First Holy Communion. The intervening instructions of the next two units will give them this opportunity.

Culminating Activity
We suggest for this unit a sand-table project, "The Stations of the Cross."[2]

---

[2]*Practical Aids for Catholic Teachers,* by Sister M. Aurelia, O.S.F., and Rev. Felix M. Kirsch (New York: Benziger Bros., 1928), pp. 232 and 264.

UNIT NINE

Content

1. Jesus Rises from the Grave.
2. Jesus Ascends into Heaven.
3. The Holy Ghost Comes upon the Apostles. The Church of Jesus Christ.

Objectives

1. To rejoice in the knowledge that Jesus arose from the grave and that one day we shall do the same.
2. To let our heart be where our treasure is, with Jesus in heaven.
3. To stimulate a longing for union with Jesus on earth through Holy Communion.
4. To know the manner in which Holy Communion is to be received.
5. To love God the Holy Ghost and the Church through which He teaches us and makes us holy.

Part One

JESUS RISES FROM THE GRAVE

Pictures

The Resurrection (Schumacher)
Emmaus (Schumacher)   *Devices*
The Apostle Thomas before Jesus

Introduction

In our last lesson we felt sad because we heard
of the sufferings and death of dear Jesus. On what *Procedure*
day did Jesus die? Yes, we call that day Good Friday
because on that day Jesus saved us from our sins.
Now I am going to tell you what happened the
following Saturday and Sunday. I think it will make
you feel happy again.

Presentation

1. Saturday was the great feast day of the Jews.
Therefore all was quiet and peaceful. The Soul of
Jesus, which had left His Body on Friday, was
gone to that place where the pious souls of Adam,
Eve, and others were waiting to be saved. Jesus
told them He had saved them by dying on the

cross. How happy they were when they heard this! How they thanked Jesus!

Saturday evening a few pious women, who were friends of Jesus, bought some expensive perfume. They wanted to go to His grave the next day and put this perfume on His Body. After awhile you and I will go with these good women to the grave of Jesus. But first we will go, all by ourselves, to the lonely spot where Jesus lies buried.

(*Show the picture.*) It is very early Sunday morning. The sun is not yet risen. All at once the earth near Jesus' grave begins to shake. An angel comes down quickly from heaven. He is as bright as the noonday sun and his garment as white as snow. Like lightning, he rolls the big stone away from the opening of the grave. Look! Jesus is alive and healthy! He rises up out of the grave! The soldiers on guard are very much afraid when they see Jesus. They run into the city to tell the Jewish leaders what had happened at the grave (Matt. 28).

2. Let us go back to the pious women. They are on their way to the grave. They are wondering how they can roll away the big stone that is over the grave of Jesus. But when they come into the garden, they see that the stone is already rolled back. They step into the open grave. There they see a young man sitting, dressed in white garments. The women

are very much afraid. It is not really a young man they see, it is an angel. The angel says to them: "Do not be afraid! You are looking for Jesus Who was crucified. He is no longer here. He is risen, as He told you. See, there is the spot where they laid Him. Go, now, and tell the disciples that He is risen. They will see Him again."

Quickly these pious women went back into the city to the disciples. Peter and John hurried at once to the grave. But they did not find Jesus. The grave was empty. Only the cloths in which they had wrapped Jesus' Body were there. The two Apostles were sad, and sadly they returned to the city.

3. That same Sunday afternoon two of the disciples made a trip out into the country. As they were walking along, a strange man caught up with them and walked along at their side. "What were you two talking about just now," said the stranger, "and why are you so sad?" The two disciples answered: "Why don't you know what has happened these past few days?" The stranger asked them what had happened, and the disciples told him the sad story about Jesus. This is the story they told: "Jesus of Nazareth had been crucified by the leaders of the Jewish people. Sunday morning some pious women went to visit the grave of Jesus. But Jesus was gone. They saw an angel at the grave,

who told them that Jesus was alive again. Two of the Apostles were also at the grave. But they, too, found it empty. Jesus was not there." When the two disciples had finished their story, the stranger said: "That is the way it had to be. The Savior had to die to open heaven."

While they were talking about these things, the three came to a house. The disciples invited the stranger to come in and spend the night with them. It was supper time and the three sat down to table. The stranger took bread into his hands and did just as Jesus had done at the Last Supper. Children, do you still remember what Jesus did with the bread at the Last Supper? Yes, He said over it: "This is My Body." And the bread was changed at once into the true Body of Jesus. The stranger did this over the bread, too. He said the same words: "This is My Body." The disciples looked at the stranger. Yes, they knew Him now. It was Jesus Himself. (*Show the picture.*) But they saw Him for only one moment. Jesus was gone! They could see Him no more!

4. The two disciples hurried back to the city where the other disciples were gathered together. All were there except Thomas. The two began to tell the story of what happened to them on their trip to the country.

As they were talking, suddenly Jesus stood there, right in front of them. He had come into the room, though the doors were locked. "Peace be to you!" It was the voice of Jesus. The disciples were very much afraid, but the Savior said to them: "It is I, do not be afraid" (Luke 24, 36 ff.). Then He showed them the wounds in His hands and feet, so that they could see it was the same Jesus Who had been nailed to the cross. Then Jesus asked them if they had anything for Him to eat. The disciples got Him a piece of fish and some honey, and Jesus started to eat. He told them, then, that it was necessary for Him to suffer as He did on the cross. All of a sudden, He was gone again.

Later Thomas came back. The disciples told him that the Lord had really risen from the grave and that He had just been with them. But Thomas said: "If I do not see the nail wounds in His hands, and if I do not put my finger into them and my hand into the wound of His side, I cannot believe it" (John 20, 24 ff.). All these things that I have just told you, children, happened on Easter Sunday.

A week later, all the disciples were gathered together again. This time Thomas was with them. Suddenly Jesus stood there before them. (*Show the picture.*) "Peace be to you!" He said, speaking to all. Then He said to Thomas: "Thomas, come here!

Put your finger into the wounds of My hand, and lay your hand into the wound of My side. Do not doubt any more, but believe." Thomas fell down upon his knees at the feet of Jesus and cried out: "O my Lord and my God!" He believed now that it was Jesus and that Jesus had really risen from the grave.

Recapitulation

1. Now let me see if you remember this story. When Jesus died on Friday, they buried His Body. Where did they put His Body? When Jesus died, His Soul left His Body. Where did His Soul go? What kind of souls were in that place where Jesus went? We call that place Limbo. Children, you know that no one, not even a very good and pious person, could get into heaven after the sin of Adam and Eve. The Savior first had to suffer for sin. The souls of bad people, of course, were sent to hell to be punished forever. But the souls of good people were sent to a place called Limbo. When Jesus died His Soul went to Limbo. The good souls there were happy when Jesus came. They were glad when Jesus told them He had saved them and that He would soon come to take them to heaven. The souls of Adam and Eve and many other good people were there in Limbo. Oh! how happy they were

when Jesus' Soul came to them. How they thanked
Jesus for having saved them!

Children, what happened on Saturday, the great
feast day of the Jews? What did some pious women
do Saturday evening? What were they going to do
with the perfume they bought? When did they go
to the grave of Jesus to do this? Did they really
anoint Jesus' Body? Why not?

When did Jesus rise from the grave? What made
His Body rise from the grave? Yes, the Soul of
Jesus, which had been with the good souls in Limbo,
went back again into His Body. That made the
Body live again, and Jesus came out of the grave.
He was shining like the sun.

2. When the pious women came to the grave,
what did they see? What did the angel say to them?
Where did they go then? Did the Apostles go to
the grave too? Which of the Apostles went to the
grave? What did they see? Did they believe right
away that Jesus was alive and that He had risen
from the grave?

3. What did two disciples do on Sunday afternoon? What happened on the way? Who came up and
walked with them? What were they speaking about?
What happened in the house? When did they know
that the stranger was their Divine Master, Jesus?
That must have been a great joy for the disciples

to have Jesus with them! Did they have that joy
of seeing Jesus for a very long time? As soon as
they knew Jesus, what happened? Where did the
disciples go then? What did they tell the Apostles?

4. Children, what happened then? What did Jesus
say to the Apostles? What did He show them? He
asked them for something to eat, and He ate what
they gave Him. Then they all believed that He was
alive. Were all the Apostles there? Who was missing? When Thomas came back, the others told him
that they had seen the Lord. What did Thomas
answer? Poor Thomas! He loved Jesus. But he
should have believed. He had seen Jesus bring people back to life; the twelve-year-old girl, the young
man they were carrying to the cemetery, and
Lazarus who was already rotting in the grave. He
should have known that the Soul of Jesus could go
back to His Body and make it live again. But he
didn't think of that. What happened, then, a week
later when Thomas was with the Apostles? What
did Jesus say to Thomas? See children! Jesus, the
Son of God, knows all things. He speaks to Thomas
and uses the very words Thomas used a week before. When Thomas saw the wounds in the hands
and side of Jesus, what did he do? what did he say?

Application   Children, we ought to be happy. Jesus lives! He will never die again! Yes, children, Jesus died to save us. He arose from His grave, that we may arise from ours and live, forever happy. Jesus teaches us that when our body dies, our soul will not die. He shows us this Himself. His Soul did not die when His Body died on the cross. Where did His Soul go? He teaches us also that our body will one day arise from the grave. He shows us that in Himself again. On the third day His Body arose from the grave. So some day our souls will go back to our bodies, and our bodies will live again.

On what day of the week did Jesus rise from the grave? Every Sunday you ought to think to yourself: Jesus rose from the dead, and one day I shall arise, too. Especially on Easter Sunday we ought to think of this with joy in our heart. On Easter we should be happy with the Church, singing and praying ALLELUJA. That means, "Praise God." Yes, we should praise God on that day because our Lord Jesus arose and because we know for certain that one day we also shall arise from the grave. But we must be good and not sin, if we want our body to be beautiful and happy when we rise from the grave. If we are not good and sin, our body will arise; but it will be punished forever. We must not do like Thomas did at first. He did not want to believe. We must believe Jesus. We must kneel at Jesus' feet and say like Thomas did later: "My Lord and my God!" When the priest holds up Jesus at Mass, we should look up at Him and say these words: "My Lord and my God!" We should do the same when the priest blesses us with Jesus at Benediction. For Jesus is our Lord and Master. He is our God.

Prayer (Practice the responses that the children make on their First Communion Day to the questions of faith put to them by the priest; or where this is not the custom, have them practice the prayers to be recited before First Holy Communion).

Activity If the children have already cut out a ciborium and host for the religion booklet have them write beneath it, "My Lord and my God."[1]

Part Two

JESUS ASCENDS INTO HEAVEN

Pictures

Devices Christ's Commission to His Apostles to Preach and Baptize

Administration of Baptism (Schumacher)

Jesus Ascends into Heaven (Schumacher)

---

[1] *Art Through Religion*, Book II, by Mary Gertrude Mc-Munigle (New York: Mentzer, Bush & Co., 1930), p. 35.

Introduction

Jesus rose from the grave on Easter Sunday. Who saw Him after He was alive again? Children, I know you felt very happy when you heard how Jesus arose from the dead. Of what did that make you think? Now today I have another story that will make you happy. I am going to tell you how Jesus went up into heaven.

Procedure

Presentation

For forty days Jesus remained on earth. He came often to visit His disciples; He wanted to tell them what they should do after He went away. One time there were five hundred people together when Jesus came (I Cor. 15, 6).

On the fortieth day after He had arisen, Jesus went with His Apostles to the Mount of Olives. The Mount of Olives, you remember, was the place where Jesus began His sufferings and where He sweat blood. When the faithful Apostles were grouped around their Master, He said to them: "Go out and teach all people. Baptize them in the name of the Father, and of the Son, and of the Holy Ghost." (*Show the picture.*) Jesus meant that the Apostles should baptize people, that is, pour water on them in the name of the Father, and of the Son, and of the Holy Ghost. Children, when you were just wee little babies, you were baptized just the way Jesus said. See! Here is a picture which shows a priest baptizing a baby as Jesus commanded. (*Show the picture and explain simply.*) And then Jesus told the Apostles they should teach all people all the things He had taught them (Matt. 28, 19, 20). But He told them to wait before going out to teach, until the Holy Ghost came upon them. The Apostles looked up at Jesus while He was speaking to them and paid attention to every word He said.

Then of a sudden Jesus began to rise up from the the ground. Higher and higher He went into the air, until· He passed through a cloud and up into heaven. The Apostles stood there in wonder, looking up at Him. Suddenly they noticed two men, clothed in white, standing beside them. They were two angels. The angels said: "Why are you looking up to heaven? Jesus, Who went up from here into heaven, will come again as you have seen Him now." (*Show the picture.*)

Children! The dear Jesus, Who suffered so much for us and died on the cross, lives again. He lives now. He is in heaven with His Body and Soul, the same Jesus Whom the Apostles saw as He left them on the Mount of Olives. He will never die again.

Recapitulation

I wonder if you remember all of this story. How long did Jesus stay on earth after Easter Sunday? Did the disciples see Him and speak to Him very often during this time? How many people were together one day when Jesus came? What did Jesus do on the fortieth day after He arose? Where did He go? What did He tell His Apostles to do? Can you tell me how a little baby is baptized? That is the way Jesus told His Apostles to baptize.

What happened after Jesus finished speaking? Where is Jesus now? Yes, Jesus is in heaven. He is in heaven — the Son of God, true God and true man, our Savior, happy and great forever with His Father. Children, whom did the Apostles see standing beside them after Jesus had gone up into heaven? What did the angels say to them? Yes, Jesus will come again on earth, looking the same as He did when He left the Apostles on the Mount of Olives. But He will come then, not as our Savior, but as our Judge, to reward or punish us as we deserve.

1. Oh, children! we will be good that Jesus may reward our soul and body with a reward that lasts *Application* forever. We will not sin. We will love Jesus and the things He wants us to believe.

2. Listen now to the story of a little boy who loved Jesus very, very much.[2] This boy's name was Tarsicius. He lived long, long ago, during those times when the Christians were hated and treated cruelly, just because they believed and loved Jesus. Often these Christians were thrown into dark and dirty prisons, where they had to wait for death. Some of them were burned alive; others were whipped to death; others had their heads cut off; still others were thrown to wild lions and tigers to be eaten up. These Christians had dug holes and tunnels in the earth, where they could hide when they went to Mass and where they could bury their dead. These underground places were called the "catacombs."

But with all this care, the Christians were often caught and dragged into prison. At the time of this story, many Christians were being held in prison, ready to die for Jesus. These brave soldiers of Christ sent a message to the bishop asking him to send them Holy Communion, for they knew that just as food makes our bodies strong, so Holy Communion strengthens our souls. They felt that if they could only receive their dear Jesus into their hearts

---

[2]Adapted from *True Stories for First Communicants*, by a Sister of Notre Dame (London: Sands & Co.; St. Louis: B. Herder Book Company, 1919).

they would be able to stand any pain for love of Him.

This message reached the bishop just as he was about to say Mass in one of the catacombs. When the Mass was over the bishop asked who would be willing to risk his life to carry Holy Communion to the prisoners. Two or three offered themselves at once, but they were too well known as Christians and the bishop was afraid they would be caught. Then a little boy named Tarsicius came up to the bishop, and kneeling at his feet begged to be allowed to carry our Lord to those who needed Him so much.

"I am so young," he said, "the pagans will think I am only a messenger boy and let me pass."

At first the bishop thought Tarsicius was too young, but the boy begged so hard to be allowed to go that the bishop at last said "Yes."

Several Sacred Hosts were placed inside a white linen cloth within a little case. Tarsicius put the little case inside his coat, just over his heart, and with his two hands clasped over his Sacred Burden, he started off. How happy he was that he could carry Jesus so close to his heart!

He was out of the catacombs now and on the public street. There he passed a group of his schoolmates who were just about to start a game. They needed only one more player, and spying Tarsicius they called to him to stop and join them.

"I am sorry," he said, "but I am on an important message."

He hurried on, but the lads caught hold of him and would not let him go.

"What have you there?" said one, seeing how tightly Tarsicius held his hands to his breast. "Let me see."

"No, no," cried the little boy, trying to free himself.

"Ah! He's a Christian," sneered one of the rough fellows. "See! He is hiding some Christian mystery there." At this the other lads became curious. They wanted to see for themselves. They struck Tarsicius and kicked him and threw him on the ground. They did their best to pull away his hands, but they could not move them. Hit him as hard as they would, the little hero would not give up Jesus.

Just at this moment a soldier, hastening toward the group, scattered them to right and left and, stooping down, lifted Tarsicius in his arms.

"Tarsicius, lad," he said, smoothing back the curls from his face.

Tarsicius opened his eyes and recognized the soldier as a Christian whom he had often seen in the catacombs.

"I am dying," said the boy, "but I have kept my God safe from them." And he handed his Precious Treasure to the soldier, who placed It reverently inside his coat. "Carry Him to the prison for me," said Tarsicius, and with a gentle sigh he fell back into the soldier's arms. His little soul was already with God, for Whom he so willingly had given his life. Little Tarsicius had shown his love for Jesus by giving Him his life.

Children, on the day of your First Holy Communion the priest is going to ask you if you really *Prayer* love Jesus. You know that if you really love Jesus, you must hate the devil and stay away from him. Do you remember that picture I showed you before of the priest baptizing a little baby? What do you call the person who is holding the baby? Yes, and the other big person is the godfather. Before the priest baptizes a little baby, he asks the baby to stay away from the devil and from sin. Of course, a little baby cannot talk; so the godparents answer for it. When you were baptized, the priest asked you these same questions and your godparents answered for you.

On your First Communion Day, you are old enough to speak for yourself. So the priest will ask you the same questions as at baptism. Here are the questions, and the answers you will give.

Priest: Do you renounce Satan?

Children: We do renounce him.

That means, children, that you promise not to have anything to do with the devil.

Priest: And all his [the devil's] works?

Children: We do renounce them.

That means you promise not to have anything to do with sin.

Priest: And all his [the devil's] pomps?

Children: We do renounce them.

Pomps are the tricks the devil uses to get you to sin. These pomps may be bad people, bad places, or bad things. You promise not to have anything to do with them.

Activity   Dramatize the story of Tarsicius.

Part Three

THE HOLY GHOST COMES UPON THE APOSTLES — THE CHURCH OF JESUS

Pictures

The Descent of the Holy Ghost upon the Apostles

Devices (Schumacher)

St. Peter Preaching on Pentecost Day

Preaching Today

Scenes from the Mass (Elevation, People's Communion)

Introduction

Before Jesus went up into heaven, He told His Apostles to go out and teach all people. But what *Procedure* did He say they should do before they went out to teach? The Apostles were very obedient. Today, we will see what they did and what happened then.

Presentation

The Apostles left the Mount of Olives and went back to the city of Jerusalem. They stayed together in a house in the city, just as Jesus wanted them to. They prayed together, too, and talked over the things that their Divine Master had told them before He went up into heaven. They were waiting now for the Holy Ghost to come to them as Jesus had promised.

(*Show the picture.*) On the tenth day after Jesus went up into heaven, the Jews had another great feast day, called Pentecost. At nine o'clock that morning, suddenly there came from heaven a noise like the sound of a strong wind. This wind blew through the whole house where the Apostles were gathered together. In the room where the Apostles were, flames of fire appeared in the shape of tongues. One of these tongues of fire rested on the head of each Apostle (Acts 2, 1 ff.). At once the Apostles were filled with the Holy Ghost; and then each one prayed to God in a different language.

When the people of Jerusalem heard the noise of the wind outside, they came running to the house of the Apostles to see what it was. Among these people were some who spoke different languages. They had come to Jerusalem from different countries for the great feast. The Apostles opened the doors of their house when they saw the great crowd of people outside. The people came into the room where the Apostles were praying and noticed that the Apostles were speaking to God in many different languages. "What is this?" they asked. "Why these men are all Galileans. How is it that we hear them talking our language?" Peter gave a sign with his hand that all should be quiet. He began to speak, as the people stood looking in wonder at him. (*Show the picture.*) "God has sent the Holy Ghost upon us," said Peter. "And now listen, O Jews, to what I tell you. Jesus Who lived among you was sent by God. He worked great wonders for you, as you know. And you have let Him be crucified. But that same Jesus has not remained in the grave. He is alive. He arose from His grave. We know that because we have seen Him. God has made Him the Lord and Savior."

Many of the people who listened to Peter saw now that they had done a very wicked thing when they crucified Jesus. They asked Peter and the other Apostles what they would have to do to make up for it. Peter said to them: "Do penance. Be baptized in the name of Jesus Christ that your sins may be forgiven." They listened to Peter, and about three thousand were baptized that day.

There were now about three thousand new people who believed in the holy teaching of Jesus. They prayed to God the Father, the Son, and the Holy Ghost. They were baptized, too, in the name of God the Father, the Son, and the Holy Ghost. All this took place on Pentecost day, the day when the Holy Ghost came upon the Apostles. The Apostles taught these people all the things Jesus had taught them; they told them all of Jesus' commandments.

Children, do you still remember how Jesus picked out seventy-two disciples? These disciples now helped the Apostles teach the people. Later on, other persons were also baptized when they heard the Apostles preach. They promised to believe the teaching of Jesus and to keep all His laws. When-

ever the Apostles preached, the people listened to
them very attentively. They obeyed the Apostles,
too, and prayed with them. The Apostles also celebrated the Holy Supper just as Jesus had done on
Holy Thursday. Jesus had told them to do this.
When we say the Apostles celebrated the Holy
Supper, we mean that they celebrated Holy Mass.

Now listen closely, children. All these people together — those who believed in Jesus and His holy
teaching and all those teachers and leaders picked
by Jesus — all these we call the Christian Church.
The house where the people and teachers came together is also called the church.

Pentecost is the birthday of the Church of Jesus.
On that day the following people belonged to the
Church: the Apostles, the seventy-two disciples, the
pious men and women who believed in Jesus while
He was alive, and the three thousand people who
had just been baptized. St. Peter was the head
Apostle. He was over all the Apostles and disciples
and people.

Today, children, the Church is made up in the
same way. The bishops take the place of the Apostles. (*Show pictures of the present and past bishops
of the diocese.*) The Pope is the head bishop. (*Show
a picture of our present Pope.*) He takes the place
of St. Peter, and like St. Peter he is the head of

the whole Church. The priests are the bishops' helpers. They take the place of the seventy-two disciples. Then come all the people who believe in Jesus and His holy teaching. The Church of Jesus will go on like that until the end of the world. Be happy that you belong to the Church of Jesus.

Recapitulation

Let us repeat what you have just learned. Where did the Apostles go after Jesus went up into heaven? What did the Apostles do in Jerusalem? How long did the Holy Ghost wait before He came upon the Apostles? What happened when He came? The tongues of fire were not the Holy Ghost. They were only a sign of the Holy Ghost. You could see the sign, but you could not see the Holy Ghost. Do you remember the time when the Holy Ghost came upon Jesus? When was it? In what shape did the Holy Ghost come upon Jesus? The dove was not the Holy Ghost. It was only a sign of the Holy Ghost. You could see the sign. So also on Pentecost day, the tongues of fire were signs of the coming of the Holy Ghost in the souls of the Apostles. What did the Apostles do when the Holy Ghost filled their souls? Did they pray to God in only one language? How then?

When the people gathered in front of the house,

what did the Apostles do? What did the people
hear when they went inside the house? In what
language were the Apostles praying? See, children,
how good God is! The Apostles were told to preach
to all people. But you know that all people do not
speak the same language. So God gave the Apostles
the gift of speaking many languages, so that they
could preach to all people.

While the crowd stood wondering at the Apostles,
what did Peter do? What did he tell the people
about Jesus? When they asked the Apostles what
they had to do, what did Peter answer? He told
them first to do penance. "You must be sorry that
you helped to kill the good, holy Jesus," he said.
"You must wish in your heart that you had not
taken part in His death. You must feel sorry for
what you did. You must believe, too, in the holy
teaching of Jesus. You must believe in God the
Father, so kind and good, Who sent His only Son
into this world for us sinners. You must believe in
the dear Son of God, Who died to save us. You
must believe in the Holy Ghost, Who wants to
make us good with His holy Love, so that we will
love only what is good and hate even the smallest
sin. You must let yourself be baptized. Then you
can hope that your sins are forgiven by this One
God in Whom there are Three Persons. The Holy

Ghost loves you as His children. He will give you happiness forever."

These words of St. Peter stirred up the people. Many of them believed. Do you know how many were baptized that day? These people who were baptized on Pentecost day promised to believe what the Apostles preached about God. They promised to do what the Apostles commanded them in the name of Jesus. They were glad to be with the Apostles. They prayed with them and celebrated the Holy Supper with them. They honored the Apostles as their fathers and as the messengers of God. Now what do you call this whole group of believers? What people made up the Church of Jesus on Pentecost day?

But the Apostles and the seventy-two disciples are no longer alive. Who takes the place of the Apostles now? Who takes Peter's place? Who takes the place of the seventy-two disciples? Today the Church of Jesus is the same as it was in the days of the Apostles. And how long did Jesus say it would last that way?

Doctrinal

1. Children, how good God is! God the Father made us, our body and soul, to be happy with Him *Application* forever in heaven. God the Son saved us. God the

Holy Ghost came upon the Apostles, and He comes to us, too, to make us holy. Oh, how happy we should be when we think of the three Persons in God! We will thank God for the many great blessings He has given us. We will love Him and please Him by doing everything He asks of us.

2. You belong to the Church of Jesus. Be glad and thank God that you belong to His Church. This Church will teach you many things. It will give you happiness forever, too. But to get this happiness, you must live a good life. You must act according to the teaching of Jesus. You must obey God and the bishops and priests of the Church of Jesus. They rule over you in God's place. You must honor your bishop just the same as you would honor one of the Apostles. Honor the priest as you would honor one of the seventy-two disciples. Obey them gladly. When they preach to you in church or in school, listen to what they say and do what they say. (*Show the picture of the priest in the pulpit.*)

Liturgical

The Apostles celebrated the Holy Supper just as Jesus did. Jesus told them to do this. Jesus also wants the bishops and priests of His Church to do the same until the end of the world. The bishops and priests do celebrate the Holy Supper every time they say Mass. Yes, children, when you go to Holy Mass, it is the same as if you were at Jesus' Last Supper or at the Holy Supper of the Apostles. And when the priest gives you Holy Communion, you take Jesus into your heart just the same as the Apostles did when Jesus Himself gave them Holy Communion. (*Show pictures of the Mass and Holy Communion.*)

Manner of Receiving Holy Communion

The manner of approaching the Communion rail and receiving Holy Communion could be practiced at this time. Regarding the act of receiving the Sacred Host, the following points should be noted: the head should be slightly back and kept quiet; the eyes downcast, but not pinched shut; the mouth moderately opened; the tongue, soft and relaxed, extended a trifle over the lower lip. After the Sacred Host has been placed on the tongue, the tongue should be drawn back slowly, the mouth closed, and the Sacred Host swallowed. These points should be demonstrated by a child previously rehearsed, and then practiced with the class.

Religious Practice

Add Eucharistic pictures to the religion booklet,

Culminating Activity

with little ejaculations like "My Lord and my God," "Jesus, I believe in You," "Jesus, I love You."

Remarks   In the instructions of this unit, only the main features of the Gospel story were given, insofar as they were needed to present the points of faith and the practice of virtue. An effort was made to couple the main events in the story with the child's daily life. Thus the recollection of the fact would be a repeated stimulation to duty. At the same time, the child's emotional powers would be warmed with holy love.

In Part Three of this unit, you will notice that the doctrine on the Church has been joined to the story of the Coming of the Holy Ghost upon the Apostles. The reasons for this are the following: (1) The union of the two topics is historically correct, for Pentecost is the birthday of the Church. (2) The Holy Ghost, Who completed the work of rehabilitating the human race, operates through the Church of Jesus Christ. (3) The close association of these two doctrines is sanctioned by their juxtaposition in the Apostles' Creed.

Though it is important to impress the union of these two doctrines upon the child's heart and pigeonhole them side by side in the little one's early historical knowledge, yet it must not be imagined that these doctrines can be presented fully at so tender an age. Hence, the nature and marks of the Church have been omitted in this instruction. Merely the broad outline of the Church has been sketched, so that the little ones might be led to a childlike submission to the Church.

UNIT TEN

Content

1. Jesus on our Altars.
2. Jesus, Give us this Food!
3. Jesus in our Hearts.

Objectives

1. To appreciate the Living Presence of Jesus in our midst.

2. To desire ardently this heavenly Food, Jesus' own Body and Blood.

3. To know what we must do before and after receiving Holy Communion.

Part One

JESUS ON OUR ALTARS

Pictures

The Multiplication of the Loaves
The Marriage Feast at Cana

Introduction

Children, we have already heard many beautiful stories about Jesus. We have heard of many good things and many great things that Jesus did. This good and great Jesus is now in heaven. But where else is He? Yes, I have often reminded you that this very minute Jesus is in our church, on the altar. Do you know how He comes there? Listen, and I shall tell you some more about it.

Presentation

1. You know, children, that Jesus can do all things. In one of our instructions I told you how Jesus fed five thousand people with five loaves of bread and two fishes. Who remembers that story? (*Show the picture and have the children tell the story.*) How great Jesus is! He can do all things. Nothing is hard for Him. Yes, children, He can also

245

change bread into His own Body. After a while I shall tell you about that, but first let us hear another story, one that you have never heard before.

2. One day Jesus went with His Apostles to a certain city called Cana. In one of the houses of Cana there was a great crowd of people gathered together for a wedding feast. (*Show the picture.*) Holy Mary was there, too. Jesus took His Apostles to this wedding feast. Everybody there was happy, eating and drinking and singing and playing. All at once Mother Mary noticed that there was no more wine for the people to drink. So she went up to Jesus and said: "They have no more wine." Mary knew that Jesus was kind and that He could do all things.

Now there were six large jugs in the room. Jesus said to the waiters: "Fill the jugs with water." And the waiters filled all six to the top. Then the Savior spoke again; "Dip it out; now you have wine." See, children! The great Jesus made wine out of water. He changed water into wine. The dear Savior can do all things. Nothing is hard for Him.

3. Yes, children, Jesus can even change wine into His own Blood; He can change bread into His own Body. Jesus does this at Holy Mass. Before the consecration there is only bread and wine on the altar. But at the consecration the priest holds the

bread and says, "This is My Body." What is the
priest holding after he says, "This is My Body"?
He then takes the chalice of wine and says, "This
is My Blood." What is in the chalice after the priest
says, "This is My Blood"? That is why the priest
always kneels down whenever he touches the Sacred
Host or the chalice after the consecration. Who can
tell me how it happens that the bread and wine become the Body and Blood of Jesus? Yes, when the
priest speaks the words of consecration, Jesus
changes the bread and wine into His own Body and
Blood. Do you know the words of consecration?
The Savior spoke them for the first time at the
Last Supper. The priest speaks these same words
at the consecration of the Mass.

Recapitulation

Now I am going to see if you remember this lesson. To what city did Jesus take His Apostles?
What was going on there? Who was present at the
wedding feast? See, children! Jesus likes to have
people enjoy a good time, as long as they stay
away from sin. What did Mary do when the wine
was all gone? Why did she tell Jesus?

There were six big jugs in the room. What did
the Savior tell the waiters to do with these jugs?
Now tell me what the Savior said after the jugs

were filled with water. Where did the wine come from? What happened to the water?

Jesus can do all things. Nothing is too hard for Him. He can even change bread into His own Body and wine into His own Blood. Where does Jesus do this? What is on the altar before the consecration? What is on the altar after the consecration? How does that happen? Who changes the bread and wine into the Body and Blood of Jesus? What does the priest do whenever he touches the Sacred Host or the chalice after the consecration? Why does he kneel down?

Application Here is a little story about the consecration of the Mass that I know you will like. One day a priest was saying Mass in the house of St. Louis, King of France. At the consecration, the priest spoke the words that Jesus used at the Last Supper — "This is my Body." Then something very wonderful happened. The priest held up the Sacred Host for the people to look at and adore. But instead of the white, shining Host, the people saw a beautiful little child in the priest's hands. How happy those people were! They could see Baby Jesus, just as holy Mary used to see Him.

Quickly one of the women ran off to tell the King. "O King," she said, "hurry, come to the chapel, and there you will see the Child Jesus in the Host."

But the King would not move.

"I know that Jesus is there," he said. "Even if I do not see Him, I believe it, because Jesus Himself has said it. That is enough for me."

See, children! The King believed that the white Host was really Jesus after the consecration. Even though it still looked like a little piece of bread, he knew it was really Jesus. Jesus Himself has said so.

When the priest holds up the white Host at Mass, we will believe that it is Jesus. Looking up at the Sacred Host, we will say: "My Lord and my God!" Then we will whisper this little prayer to Jesus. "Jesus, I believe in You. I hope in You. I love You." And when the priest lifts up the golden chalice, we will believe that it holds the holy Blood of Jesus. Again we will say as we look up: "My Lord and my God!" Then we will whisper this prayer to Jesus. "O Jesus, let Your holy Blood come over my soul and make it pure."

Children, keep very quiet during this most sacred time. Jesus is on the altar. How happy you should be that He is so near! He is looking at you, looking right into your very heart. He loves you. He wants to come to you. Yes, He will come to you very soon.

Prayer   Repeat and rehearse simply the prayers to be
said before Holy Communion.

              When Jesus comes, there are certain things you
Religious   must have ready and certain things you must do. I
Practice   will write them out for you.

Before Holy Communion

   1. No eating nor drinking after midnight — twelve
o'clock.
   2. Your soul must be free from mortal sin.
   3. Prayers to Jesus.

At Holy Communion.

   1. Fold your hands and keep your eyes down.
   2. Think only of Jesus.
   3. Put your tongue out, not very far. Have your
head back a little.
   4. Swallow the Sacred Host. Do not touch It with
your finger.

After Holy Communion.

   1. No looking around. Jesus is with you.
   2. Prayers to Jesus.

              Letter cutting — mount letters for religion book-
Activity   let. "This is My Body." "This is My Blood."

              (Perhaps the children could cut a circle from
white construction paper; place beneath it the
words, "This is My Body." A chalice may likewise
be cut, etc.)

Part Two

JESUS, GIVE US THIS FOOD!

Picture

A Ciborium

Devices

Eucharistic Symbols

Wheat and Grapes

Introduction

Children, I am sure you still remember the story of how Jesus fed five thousand people with five loaves of bread and two fishes. How did these five thousand people feel after Jesus had fed them? Now I am going to tell you what happened the next day.

Procedure

Presentation

The morning after that wonderful supper, the people ate the leftover pieces for breakfast. Then they set out to look for the Savior. He was not there any more, and they had to look and look until finally they found Him in the city of Capharnaum. Do you know why they were so anxious to find Him? The bread which Jesus had blessed and given to them tasted so good, that they wanted very much to eat some more of it. The Savior knew that and said to them: "Ah, yes, you want some more of that good bread for your body. But you ought to be looking for a better kind of food, a food for your soul." Then the people cried out: "Lord! Give us this food for our soul." And Jesus answered: "I am the Bread of Life, the food of your soul. He who eats this food, will live forever. My Flesh is this food. My Blood is this drink for your soul."

Children, do you know where this Food of our souls is kept? Yes, in the tabernacle, behind the little golden door. You have seen the priest come down to the Communion rail to give people this heavenly Food. Notice that the priest holds in his hand a golden cup shaped almost like the chalice used at Mass. This golden cup is called a ciborium. *(Show the picture.)* It is from the ciborium that the priest gives you the food of your soul, Jesus, the Bread of Life, each time you go to Holy Communion. Very soon now you will receive this heavenly Food for the first time. How happy you should be! Count the days and then count the hours. Ask Jesus to help you make your heart beautiful and golden like the ciborium.

O children! If the blessing of Jesus made ordinary bread so good and so sweet, then how sweet

and good must be the very Body and Blood of Jesus
Himself.

(*Show the symbols of the Holy Eucharist, the
wheat and grapes.*) Here are wheat and grapes.
From wheat we make bread, and from grapes we
make wine. Bread is a food for our body. Wine is
a drink for our body. But Jesus changes bread into
His Body and wine into His Blood. The Body and
Blood of Jesus is the food and drink of our soul.
How good Jesus is to give us His own Body for our
food and His blood for our drink! How strong and
good they ought to make our soul! O dear Savior,
give us this Food very soon!

Recapitulation

When the people lost Jesus after He had fed
them with five loaves of bread and two fishes, where
did they finally find Him? Why were they so anxious to find Jesus? Jesus knew that they wanted
more bread, but what did He tell them? What
other kind of bread should they be looking for?
When the people asked the Savior for this food for
the soul, what did He say to them?

Who can tell me where this Food of our souls is
kept? What do you call the golden cup from which
the priest gives us this heavenly Food? How can a
little child make his heart beautiful like the golden

ciborium? Of what do the wheat and the grapes remind you? When you think of this heavenly Food, how should you feel in your heart? What prayer should a little child say that reminds you of the prayer of the people whom Jesus fed long ago? (*Desire.*) Dear Jesus, I will try to please You, because You are so good to me. (*Repeat several times in unison.*)

Application Now I have a beautiful story to tell you of a wee little girl whose name was Marie.[1] This story happened many years ago during the time of a great war. One night the soldiers sent word to the people of a certain town that they would stop there overnight and would sleep in the church, which was the only large building in the village.

When the people heard this they were in great trouble. The priest was not at home and many of these soldiers were wicked men, and it would not have been right to leave Jesus in the tabernacle where the soldiers might insult Him. What were they to do?

Now you know that no one but a priest or deacon should take the Blessed Sacrament in his hands except in case of need. No one should touch the cibo-

[1]Adapted from *True Stories for First Communicants,* by a Sister of Notre Dame (London: Sands & Co; St. Louis: B. Herder Book Company, 1919).

rium in which Jesus is kept without special permission. But when the soldiers were going to sleep in the church, it was, of course, "a case of need." Yet not one of the villagers dared to take the ciborium away. First they asked the sacristan who cleaned the church, but he said "No." They asked one man after the other, but each was afraid or said he was not good enough. What was to be done?

At last one of the men said: "I know what to do. My little girl Marie is four years old. She is good and innocent, just like an angel. I will take her up to the altar. She shall take our Savior from the tabernacle, and then we will carry her to the priest's house, while she holds the ciborium in her baby hands."

Slowly and reverently her father carried her up the altar steps, and unlocked the tabernacle door. Lovingly Marie drew out the ciborium which held her dear Savior and pressed it to her breast. Her little heart beat fast while she whispered to Jesus how pleased she was to have Him in her arms. Tighter and tighter she clasped the white silk veil which covered our Lord's little golden house. Tighter and tighter her father held his little girl in his arms, for she was holding in her tiny hands the great Lord and God Who made us all.

All the villagers followed Marie and her father.

This made quite a long procession. At last they came to the priest's house. There Jesus was kept safely all night, the good people taking turns to kneel on guard before Him.

Children, do you know why Marie was chosen instead of one of the men for the great honor of carrying Jesus? It was because she was so innocent and pure. She had never committed any sin, as she was only four years old, and so had never offended dear Jesus. It is into pure and innocent hearts like hers that Jesus wishes to come in Holy Communion.

Very soon, when the priest came back, the people told him all that they had done. He was very pleased and told Marie that she must always remember what a great honor she had had, and that she must begin to prepare her heart to become a home for the same dear Jesus Whom she had carried in her hands.

WHAT A LITTLE BOY AND GIRL SHOULD LEARN
FROM THIS STORY

1. Jesus is very great and very holy.

2. Jesus wants our hearts to be holy, free from any big sin, when He comes in Holy Communion.

Prayer

Practice the acts Before and After Holy Communion. Keeping Jesus company after He has come into our hearts should be stressed. The manner in which the people kept watch during the night, taken from the foregoing story, could be used to explain this.

Returning from the Communion rail like little *Religious Practise*
Maries.

Crayon Drawing for religion booklet. — Grapes *Activity*
and Wheat.

Part Three

JESUS IN OUR HEARTS

Pictures

Jesus Friend of Children (Schumacher)   *Devices*
Jesus Crucified (Schumacher)

Introduction

Who can tell me how many days are left before First Communion? Soon you can count the hours. *Procedure* Yes, I know you are happy, because Jesus is coming very soon. Your little heart beats fast every time you think of His coming. Today, children, I am going to show you two pictures. You have seen them before, but I want you to look at them and think about them again.

Presentation

1. This is the picture you saw in your first instructions, Jesus Friend of Children. (*Show the picture*

*and have the children look at it quietly and care-
fully.*) Jesus preached many holy words to the
people. He did many wonderful things, too, that
you still remember. What did He do to the blind
man? What did He do to the man who was deaf
and dumb? What did He do to many people who
were sick? Yes, He even made three dead persons
live again. See, how great the Savior is! He is God.

But great as He was, He still loved children. He
would not let the Apostles send them away, even
though He was tired. He put His hand kindly on
the little one's head and blessed him. He wanted
all the children to come up close to Him.

That same great Jesus is going to come to you,.
too. He is not only going to put His hand on your
head and bless you, He is not only going to let you
crawl up close to Him. No, He is coming into your
very heart. What a great honor! Jesus, Who worked
so many wonders; Jesus, Who is God — coming to
poor little me. O wonderful thing! A poor little
child receives in his mouth and in his breast his
God and Lord.

2. Now children, let us look at another picture
— Jesus hanging on the cross. On what day did
Jesus suffer and die on the cross? What is the name
of the place where Jesus suffered and died? Now
children, who can tell me some of the pains our

Savior suffered when He was hanging on the cross? They were pains much worse than any toothache, and Jesus had them all over His Body.

See how much Jesus loved us! He suffered all that for us. He could have come down from the cross. But He did not want to. He wanted to suffer all those hurts and pains for us. Look at the crucifix. See the arms of Jesus stretched out wide on the cross! So much He loved us; not just a little (*extend the arms a little*), not this much (*extend them wider*), but very, very much (*extend them as Jesus has them on the cross*).

Now tell me how much you love Jesus. (*Have the children open their arms by degrees till they are stretched out wide.*) So much.

Dear children! This same Jesus is coming into your hearts. When He comes, imagine that your heart is Calvary. The cross with Jesus all-bleeding is planted there. The holy Blood of Jesus is dripping, dripping down upon your heart.

Prayer

Jesus, we thank You. You are the true Son of God. You suffered so many pains for us. You died on the cross, with arms stretched wide, to show us how much You loved us. You died to take away our sins. You died that we might go to heaven.

Jesus, we thank You. Yes, we will love You with all our heart. We will obey You and Your Father in heaven. We will obey You now and always. Help us to keep every word of this promise.

Recapitulation

Children, when Jesus comes into your heart in Holy Communion, of what two pictures of Jesus are you going to think? Tell me some of the great things that Jesus did, some of the wonders that He worked. Did Jesus love children? Does He love you? What an honor that this great Jesus is coming to you! Though you are only a little child, your Lord and God is coming to you. What did Jesus do to the little children of long ago when their mothers brought them to Him? All that, He will do to you.

Of what other picture of Jesus are you going to think? What do all the sufferings and pains of Jesus tell us about Him? What else shows us how much Jesus loved us when He died on the cross? What will your heart be like when Jesus comes? Then the holy Blood of Jesus will flow over your heart. What will It do to your heart? What little prayer will you say to Jesus? Jesus, we thank You. Jesus, we love You. Jesus, we will obey You.

Application   Long ago there lived in a country far away from here a little girl whose name was Imelda. When she

was only eleven years old she went to live with the
Sisters in the convent. She was a very holy child.
She did many hard things, penances we call them,
to please Jesus. Imelda especially liked to kneel
before the tabernacle and say her prayers to the
Savior.

This little girl, however, had not yet received her
First Holy Communion. In those days, children
were not allowed to go to Holy Communion as early
in their life as you are. But Imelda was very anxious
to receive Jesus. She asked the priest time and time
again if she might not make her First Holy Communion. But the priest told her she would have to
wait until she was a little older. Poor Imelda! How
could she wait any longer for the coming of dear
Jesus?

One day all the Sisters were present at Mass.
Little Imelda was there too. When the little bell
rang at Communion time, all the Sisters walked
slowly with folded hands up to the Communion
rail. The little child was left alone. She was the
only one in the church who could not receive her
Savior into her heart. She saw the priest passing
up and down the rail, giving the Sacred Host to
each of the Sisters. Oh, how very much she wanted
to be there too. "Jesus, dear Jesus," she whispered
as a tear fell down her cheek, "there is only one

thing I want on this earth. Come into my heart! That is all I ask."

At this same moment, a Sacred Host was seen coming from above. Closer and closer It came, until It rested over the head of little Imelda. The priest saw what had happened. Hurrying to the place where Imelda was kneeling, he reverently took the Sacred Host; and knowing now that Jesus wanted to go to this holy child, he placed It on her tongue.

In this wonderful way Blessed Imelda received her First Holy Communion. From this you can learn how much Jesus loves to come to little children when their hearts are pure and holy. Tell Jesus how happy you are that He is soon coming to you. Say to Him: Come, Lord Jesus, come! (*Repeat in unison.*)

Culminating Activity   Religion booklet — Cut out and paste a picture of Jesus — and letter below "Come, Lord Jesus, come!"

Remarks   This Unit is planned as the immediate preparation for First Communion Day. The lessons are not so much an appeal to the intellect as to the heart of the child. They are intended to be inspirational talks about the Real Presence and the dispositions necessary for the proper reception of Holy Communion. Devotion and desire have been the main objectives in the presentation of material.

UNIT ELEVEN

Content

1. Summary: First Part of the Apostles' Creed.
2. Summary: Second Part of the Apostles' Creed.
3. Summary of the Commandment of Love: The Our Father and the Hail Mary.
4. General Repetition.

Objectives

1. To put before our minds and hearts the main points of the year's instructions.

2. To join the teachings of faith with the principal prayers we recite, namely, the Apostles' Creed, Our Father, and Hail Mary, so that our prayers may remind us of the teachings of faith, and the teachings of faith, in turn, may give us food for thought during prayer.

3. To stir up love and gratitude toward God for all His gifts, especially the Holy Eucharist.

Part One

SUMMARY: FIRST PART OF THE APOSTLES' CREED

Pictures

God the Creator (Schumacher)
Jesus in the Manger (Schumacher)
Jesus on the Cross (Schumacher)
Jesus in Heaven

Devices

Introduction

Now children, I want to see if you have remembered what I have told you about the good God. I shall repeat the main things we have learned in our past instructions. That will help you to remember them better. These things will make you happy, they will help you to lead good, pious lives.

Procedure

Presentation

1. Children, who made me? Who made you? your parents? the earth and all that is on earth? the heavens and all things in the sky and in heaven? Yes, as soon as God willed something to be there, it was there right away. If God wants to make some-

thing now, all He has to do is will it and it is made at once. That is why we say: God made all things. He can make whatever He wills. So we say: God is the almighty or all-powerful Creator. When we pray the Apostles' Creed we say: *I believe in God the Father almighty, Creator of heaven and earth.* Repeat this, children. (*Show the picture.*)

Who was the first man God made? the first woman? First He made their bodies. These bodies were not alive, so what did God put into them to make them alive? Whom did God create in the heavens? How did God act toward these angels? Where were they when God created them? How did they get along there? Children, how did God act toward Adam and Eve? Where did He place them? How did they get along in Paradise? And how does God act toward us? He gives us, too, a body and a soul, and everything that we need to live and make us happy. He gives us His own Body to be the food of our soul. That is God's greatest gift to us. The dear, good God!

God was very good to the angels. He gave them many things to make them happy. How do you think they should have acted toward God? God gave Adam and Eve many nice things, too. How should they have acted? He also gives us all many things to make us happy. How should we act toward Him?

How could the angels please God? Yes, by doing whatever He told them. What should Adam and Eve have done to please God? What must we do to please Him? Did all the angels please God by obeying Him always? No, many wanted to do just as they liked. How were they when they no longer wanted to do as God said but only as they liked? Were they still good then? No, they were bad, very bad. What did God do with these bad angels? Where did He put them? And how are these bad angels getting along there?

Did the first people, Adam and Eve, always please God by obeying Him? What command did God give them? They disobeyed that command. Who whispered to them to disobey? How were they after they disobeyed God? Where was God when they disobeyed? Did He know what they did? Where is God? How much does God know? What did God do to Adam and Eve when they were bad? Yes, God rewards the good and punishes the bad.

Now children, how do we please God? If we do what God commands, we love God. Then God loves us. Does God know when we obey Him? Does He love us then? and reward us, too? We love God when we obey Him. If we are bad and do what God said we should not do, is He near us then? Do we love Him then? Are we happy about Him or are we afraid of Him when we have done bad? What does God do to us when we are bad?

Children, you ought to be happy to think of the good God. He is with you everywhere and knows everything you do. Please Him by doing what He tells you. He will love you and reward you for it. You will love Him also, and you will be happy. If you disobey God, He sees that you do not love Him. He will not love you either and He will punish you. Remember! God is everywhere. He knows all things. Always be afraid to disobey Him.

2. Do you still know how many people were hurt by the sin of Adam and Eve? Were we hurt too? Yes, your mother has to suffer and have sorrow with her children, just like Eve. We must all work hard and sweat, like Adam. Like Adam and Eve, we must all die. We also got something else from Adam and Eve: being bad and not wanting to obey God. We are all bad in the eyes of God. We come into the world with sin on our soul. If God had not helped us, not one of us could go to heaven. God promised to send Someone to help us. Who was that One? This Redeemer was to bring us forgiveness of sins, love of God, help in being good, and happiness forever. The Redeemer and Savior promised by God has already come into the world. Who is our Redeemer? In the Apostles' Creed we

pray: (*I believe*) *in Jesus Christ, His* (*that is, the Father's*) *only Son, our Lord.* Repeat this. Now take the first two parts together.

3. Now tell me, children, where was the Redeemer born? What is the name of His holy Mother? Who told her that she would be the Mother of the Redeemer? What did the angel say to the Virgin Mary? What did the angel promise her she should have? What name should this Son have? Who would come upon Holy Mary? Whose Son would this Child be? Where was this Son born to Mary? In the Apostles' Creed we say: *Who was conceived by the Holy Ghost, born of the Virgin Mary.* Repeat this last part and then take the three parts together. (*Show the picture.*)

Where was the Savior born? Who first heard the news that He was come on earth? Who told the shepherds? Were there other people living far away from Bethlehem who found out about the Savior's birth? How did these men find out? Where did Mary and Joseph take Jesus when He was forty days old? Who saw Jesus there and said that He was the Savior of the world? What do you know about Jesus when He was twelve years old? What happened there? What did Jesus tell Holy Mary when she said that she and Joseph had been looking for Him? He wanted to speak and hear about

His Father. Who was the Father about Whom Jesus spoke? See, children, Jesus calls Himself the Son of God.

4. When Jesus was thirty years old He began to preach. But what did He first let St. John the Baptist do to Him? Who remembers what happened while Jesus was being baptized? Who came down upon Him? Whose voice was heard coming from heaven? Now, how many persons are there in God? what are the names of these three Persons? When we make the sign of the cross, we say . . .

How many years did Jesus preach? He also did very many kind deeds to the people. Tell me some of the wonders the Savior worked on sick people? on three people who were dead? O great, kind Jesus! What happened after Jesus had been teaching three years? What did some bad people plan to do to Him? Who helped these bad men, so that they were able to take the Savior prisoner on the sly? After the high priests said that Jesus had to die, to whom did they take Him? Did Jesus have to suffer much there? What did Pontius Pilate tell the soldiers to do to Him? Oh! how that cruel scourging hurt Him. What else did the soldiers do to hurt our Lord? How did they make fun of Him? Oh! the poor Savior.

After Pilate gave permission to crucify Jesus,

where did they take Him? Where did He have to carry His cross? But He was too weak to carry the cross alone, so they forced a stranger to help Him. On Calvary they nailed the Savior to the cross. They made fun of Him, too, while He was hanging there. Oh, what terrible pains Jesus had to suffer on Calvary! At three o'clock in the afternoon Jesus died. Then His Body was buried. In the Apostles' Creed we pray: *Suffered under Pontius Pilate, was crucified, died and was buried.* Repeat that, children. (*Show the picture.*)

Who was it that suffered? Who was crucified? Who died? Who was buried? Whose Son is Jesus? Yes, God the Son suffered, was crucified, died and was buried. Who allowed the Jews to crucify Jesus? Under whom, then, did Jesus suffer? Why did the dear Savior suffer so much? Why did He die? Yes, He suffered and died for us. He suffered and died because all people, from Adam on, are sinners. He did it all because the sin of Adam and Eve came upon us and because He wanted to take that sin away.

Jesus saved us! He, the Son of God, took our punishment away through His sufferings and death. Now we can go to heaven again. Children, you will love Jesus, will you not? You will love Him because He suffered such bitter pains for all of us and opened heaven again for us. God the Father created us all. Who redeemed or saved us? Yes, God the Son, Jesus Christ.

You remember, too, what Jesus did for us on the Thursday before He died. He wanted to live in our churches. He wanted to come into our hearts. So He changed bread and wine into His Body and Blood. Then He told His Apostles to do the same, and the priests, too. The priest brings Jesus down on the altar when he says Mass; he puts Jesus into our hearts when he gives us Holy Communion.

5. Tell me, children, what happens to a person when he dies? The soul leaves the body. Does the soul die too? The dead Body of Jesus was buried. Where did His Soul go when It left His Body? On the third day where did His Soul come again? When the Body of Jesus became alive again, did He stay in the grave? What happened? To whom did the Savior come after He arose from the dead? Who else saw Him after He was alive again? But the people did not only see Jesus. Thomas even touched the very wounds in His hands and side. One time, too, Jesus ate with His disciples. How many people saw Jesus one day? In the Apostles' Creed we pray: *He descended into hell (Limbo); the third day He arose again from the dead.* Repeat.

6. Jesus remained forty days with His disciples and spoke to them many times after He arose from the dead. Where did He go with them on the fortieth day? From where did He ascend into heaven? In heaven Jesus now enjoys all power and glory with His Father. We pray in the Apostles' Creed: *He ascended into heaven, sitteth at the right hand of God the Father almighty.* Repeat. (*Show the picture.*)

7. Oh, children, how happy we are! Dear Jesus, Who loves us so much, Who suffered so very much for us, lives up there in heaven. He lives! He rules over the world with His Father forever! He loves us! He cares for us! And some day He will take us up to heaven with Him. He loves us and cares for us, too, from His little house on the altar. When He comes into our heart, He helps to get it ready for heaven.

Children, will Jesus come again to this earth looking as He did when He was here before? What did the two angels tell the Apostles about Jesus after He had left them on the Mount of Olives? Why will Jesus come a second time to this earth? That is why we pray in the Creed: *From thence He shall come to judge the living and the dead.* Repeat.

Recapitulation

Now children, listen carefully. This is how we pray the Apostles' Creed.

I believe in God the Father almighty, Creator of heaven and earth.

When we say these words we think of this: There is one God Who made all things. He made heaven and earth and all things in heaven and on earth. He made the sun, the moon, and the stars. He made the mountains, trees, and animals. He made you and me and all the angels in heaven. He can make whatever He wants. The clouds, wind, lightning, hail, and all things obey Him. We must obey Him, too, because He is our Lord. We must love Him because He created us and gives us so many good things now and because He will give us many more good things in heaven. We should say to Him: Dear, good Father! We must look to Him alone to protect us, to help us, to save us.

And (I believe) in Jesus Christ His only Son, our Lord.

Here we think that the good God had an only Son Who loved us so much that He became man for us. His name is Jesus Christ. He taught us how to be good and how to please God. We must love

Jesus and be obedient to Him too. We must honor Him as the Son of God just the same as we honor God the Father.

Who was conceived by the Holy Ghost, born of the Virgin Mary.

We believe that this Son of God, Who wanted to become man for us and live on earth among us, chose the holy, most pious Virgin Mary to be His Mother. Holy Mary received Jesus as her Son through the almighty power of the Holy Ghost, the third Person of God.

Suffered under Pontius Pilate, was crucified, died and was buried.

Here we think of all that the Son of God suffered to save us. He suffered under Pontius Pilate. He took our punishment on Himself. He did this to save us from the sin that came on our soul from Adam and to save us from the sins we ourselves do. He did this to save us from the punishment we deserve for our sins. Here are some of the things Jesus suffered for us: He was scourged, crowned with thorns, made fun of, and died on the cross. Then His Body was buried. Oh, children, we ought to love this dear Jesus with all our heart. We ought to live as He taught us. We should be glad that He suffered the punishment of sin in our place.

Thank Him for His love. With all your heart hate sin which alone made Jesus suffer as He did. Try very hard never to sin again.

He descended into hell, the third day He arose again from the dead.

We believe this, children. We should be happy with those good people in Limbo to whom Jesus brought that good news of His death on the cross. They could not go to heaven before Jesus died for sin. When Jesus came to them, they were, of course, very happy. Later they went with the dear Savior to heaven to be happy forever. Be glad that the dear, divine Savior lives now. Yes, He will live forever. He will lead us also to heaven where we will be happy forever.

He ascended into heaven, sitteth at the right hand of God the Father almighty.

We also believe that our dear Redeemer lives in heaven and rules over the whole world with God the Father. We know that He loves us from heaven. He will help us to live good lives as He taught. We can be happy forever through Him and with Him.

From thence He shall come to judge the living and the dead.

We believe what Jesus told the high priest just before He was crucified: You will see the Son of

Man coming in the clouds of heaven with power and glory. We believe what the angels told the Apostles after Jesus had ascended into heaven: Jesus, Who has been taken from you up into heaven, will come again just as you have seen Him now. We believe that one day Jesus will come down from heaven, that He will be seen in the clouds with great power and glory. We do not know what year, what day, what hour He will come. But we do know for sure that He will come to judge all men. He died to save all, the good and the bad. He will also judge all. Adam and Eve will be there. So will all those who are alive when He comes. And all those who died from the time of Adam and Eve until the end of the world will be there. Children, we believe this. That is why we ought to be good. We must live just as Jesus taught us. We must try to live as He lived. Then, when He comes to judge us, He will see that we are His good children and He will take us with Him into heaven.

(*Drill the Apostles' Creed from the beginning to the words, "He will come to judge the living and the dead."*) Children, these words of the Apostles' Creed tell what you believe. So learn them well.

Rehearse: the sign of the cross, the genuflection, folding of hands.

Religious Practice

Part Two

SUMMARY: SECOND PART OF THE APOSTLES' CREED

Pictures

Devices

Descent of the Holy Ghost (Schumacher)
Feed My Lambs, Feed My Sheep (Schumacher)
The Saints in Heaven

Introduction

Procedure

So far, children, you have told me what we believe about God the Father and God the Son. But you also know quite a bit about the third Person of God, the Holy Ghost.

Presentation

You remember that the Angel Gabriel came to the holy virgin, Mary. He spoke to her, didn't he? From Whom would Mary receive the Son of God as her Child? Who came upon Jesus in the form of a dove when He was baptized by John? Whom did Jesus promise at the Last Supper to send to His Apostles? Before Jesus ascended into heaven, He told the Apostles to wait for Someone and not to preach until that One came. Who was that One? When did the Holy Ghost, the third Person of God, come upon the Apostles? The Holy Ghost did not come upon them in the form of a dove as He did upon Jesus. In what form did He come upon them? What could the Apostles do as soon as the Holy Ghost came into their hearts? Children, the Holy Ghost makes us good and holy, just as He made the Apostles good and holy. That is why we pray in the Apostles' Creed: *I believe in the Holy Ghost.* Repeat. (*Show the picture.*)

God the Father created us. God the Son redeemed us. God the Holy Ghost makes us holy. Yes, children, we believe in the Holy Ghost. We must try to live a holy life. We must love and do only what is good. We must hate and stay away from what is bad. God the Holy Ghost will help us do that if we just pray to Him for it. But He cannot love us if we are bad and want to stay bad, because He is the *Holy* Ghost.

You also know, children, that after the coming of the Holy Ghost, Peter preached to the people. That very day many people believed in Jesus. How many people were baptized that day? What do we call all those people who really believed in Jesus and were baptized? Yes, the Church of Jesus. Whom did Jesus make the leaders and teachers of His Church? Who was picked to be the head of the Apostles? (*Show the picture.*) Who were the Apostles' helpers? The Apostles and the disciples were the teachers, and the other people who believed in Jesus obeyed them. Who takes the place of the Apostles now? Who is now the head of all the bishops? Who takes the place of the seventy-two disciples?

The Church of Jesus is still made up of the teachers and the rest of the people who believe. All of us who believe here on earth and all the good people who are dead have a part in the good things of the Church. We love one another and pray for one another. I love you and pray for you, children. You must love me and pray for me. And all of us must love the people who are dead and we must pray for them. In the Apostles' Creed we pray: (*I believe*) *in the holy Catholic Church, the Communion of Saints*. Repeat.

Children, we must try to be good and pious children of this Church. Remember, the Church of Jesus teaches people everywhere in the world just what Jesus taught and what the Apostles preached. The Pope, the bishops, and the priests are the teachers of the Church of Jesus today. We must believe what they teach us. We must do what they tell us about the commands of God. I told you some time ago what the Apostle Peter said to the people on the day the Holy Ghost came upon the Apostles.

They had asked Peter what they should do. Peter said: "Do penance and be baptized in the name of Jesus Christ that your sins may be forgiven." Peter promised that their sins would be forgiven if they did penance and were baptized in the name of Jesus Christ.

You were baptized in the name of Jesus soon after you were born. When you were baptized, God took away the sin that came upon your soul from Adam. But what happened if you let new sins come upon your soul? Could they be taken away? Yes, Jesus gave His Church the power to take away these sins if you do penance and are sorry for them. These sins are forgiven when you go to confession. The Church of Jesus can take away all our sins. This is what we mean when we say in the Apostles' Creed: (*I believe*) *in the forgiveness of sins.* Repeat.

God is very good. Jesus is very forgiving. He takes away our sins if we are really sorry and do better. Remember, God forgave Adam and Eve as soon as they were sorry for their sin. So He will forgive us. Of course, you should try not to do what God has forbidden. Do what He tells you. But if it should happen that you do something that God hates, that is, if you commit sin, remember that in the Church of Jesus you can have these sins taken off your soul. You know how, don't you? In confession, of course. Oh, how good it is to be a Catholic, a child of the Church of Jesus.

We believe that Jesus will come back to this earth from heaven to judge the good and the bad. What will happen to the bodies that are in their graves on that day when Jesus will come to judge all people? Who said so? Yes, children, Jesus said the hour will come when all who are in the grave will hear the voice of the Son of God. They will arise from the grave. Those who were good will arise to receive their reward, those who were bad will arise to receive their punishment.

Yes, the bodies of all shall arise from the grave. Jesus arose from His grave on Easter morning, as you remember; and as He arose, so we also will arise. How happy that should make us if we are good! How terrible if we are bad! Repeat this with me, children; our bodies will all arise from the grave. That is what we mean when we pray: (*I believe in*) *the Resurrection of the body.* Repeat.

The souls and bodies of the good people will then go up to heaven, just as Jesus went up into heaven with Body and Soul. The bodies and souls of the bad people, those who were not sorry and who died with big sins on their soul, will go to hell. The good will stay forever in heaven; the bad will have to stay forever in hell. The good people will always be happy. They will have every kind of happiness and never any suffering. But the bad people will always be unhappy. They will have every kind of suffering and never any happiness. We believe in this when we pray: (*I believe in*) *life everlasting.* Repeat. (*Show the picture.*)

Children, this life of never-ending happiness we will receive if we are good, if we love God and obey Him, if we love our neighbor and do good to him. Thank the dear God for being so kind to us. Always be afraid to do anything bad against the good, holy God. If we are bad and stay bad, remember that God will punish us and we will be unhappy forever and ever.

Recapitulation

Remember well the things I just told you. I said: *I believe in the Holy Ghost.*

That means: I believe in the third Person of God. The Holy Ghost, the third Person of God, came upon Jesus in the form of a dove. He came upon the Apostles in the form of tongues of fire. The same Holy Ghost makes us holy, too, even though we do not see Him. He made us holy the first time when we were baptized.

The holy Catholic Church, the Communion of Saints.

I believe in the holy Church of Jesus. That Church is spread over the whole earth under the teaching of the Pope, bishops, and priests. That Church believes everything that Jesus taught, everything that the Apostles preached, everything that the Pope and bishops teach today. I am very happy that all the people who belong to the Church of Jesus are united to one another and tha, they all have a part in the many blessings of the Church. I will always stay a Catholic. I will live and die as a child of this Church of Jesus. I will always obey our bishop and priests.

Forgiveness of Sins.

I believe that in this holy, Catholic Church, I can have the sin which comes on my soul from Adam forgiven in baptism. The sins that I myself commit can be forgiven, too, in confession.

Resurrection of the Body.

I believe that when Jesus Christ comes to judge all people, He will awaken our bodies from their graves. He will make us arise with the same flesh and blood that we now have. Then He will judge us about all the things we have done in this life with our bodies and souls. So I will use my body now only to do good.

And Life Everlasting.

I believe that after Jesus judges us all at the end

of the world, our souls and bodies will live forever, they will never have an end. The good people will be happy forever in heaven, the bad will be unhappy forever in hell.

This, children, is the belief of the holy, Catholic Church. Now let us all pray the Apostles' Creed together. I will say the words first and you repeat them after me. You must all know this prayer by heart. Be sure, too, to pray it often and with devotion.

I believe in God . . . life everlasting. Amen.

Amen. That means: Yes, that is true; I believe that, and I will always believe it as long as I live. (*Drill this part and then the entire Creed.*)

Rehearse: the small sign of the cross; raising the hat or bowing when passing the church or meeting priest or religious; striking the breast.   *Religious Practice*

Part Three

SUMMARY OF THE COMMANDMENT OF LOVE: THE OUR FATHER AND THE HAIL MARY

Pictures

Child at Prayer

Jesus Teaches the Our Father (Schumacher)   *Devices*

Picture of the Blessed Virgin

Introduction

Let me see, children, if you can still remember
Procedure something I told you quite a while ago. The dear
Lord Jesus preached to the people for three years.
Some of the things He taught, you have already
told me. But now I want to see if you remember a
few more of His teachings.

Presentation

1. Jesus liked to preach about His Father. He
told us how much His Father loves us. What does
the dear God give us because He loves us? Who
created everything that we need for food, drink,
and clothing? From Whom, then, do we receive all
things? What did Jesus say we have to do if we
want to receive the things we need from God? Jesus
pointed to the birds and flowers — and what did
He say? Who sent Jesus, the Son of God, into this
world? Why did He come? What did He want to
do for us poor sinners who deserved punishment?
To save us and take away this punishment, what
did the Son of God have to do? Yes, the dear Jesus
loved us so much that He suffered and died for us.
Do you think God the Father loved us when He
gave us His only Son? Who still remembers the
words of Jesus about that? God loved the world so

much that He . . . . Why did He give us His Son? Yes, that all who believe in Him might not be lost, but that they might have life forever.

God loves us very much. What should we do for Him then? Can you tell me the words of Jesus about this? What did Jesus say to the man who asked Him this question: "Master, which is the greatest commandment?" Jesus said: "Love! Love God, your Lord, with your whole soul and with your whole heart." Woe to the one who does not love God, the good, kind God Who loves us so much! But blessed is the child who loves God with his whole soul. Children, we ought to be glad when we think about God. We ought to try hard to please Him. When you learn about Him in your instructions be happy. When your parents pray with you at home be glad to pray along. When you are in church pray nicely and think of God and tell Him that you want to love Him very much. Pray to Him when you get up in the morning, pray to Him before and after you eat your meals, pray to Him at night before you go to bed. (*Show the picture.*) If you do that you will please God. Two more things you should do to show you love God: go to Mass every Sunday and Holyday, and never eat meat on Friday.

Another thing. Whatever God asks, you ought

to do gladly. That is the way you please God too. What should you do when your parents tell you something? You ought to obey God the same way. He wants you to obey your parents, so obey them out of love for God. He wants you to obey the priest and your teachers, so obey them out of love for God. He wants you to learn your lessons well in school, so do that also out of love for Him. He wants you to be kind to your brothers and sisters, not to quarrel with them or hurt them; so be kind to them out of love for Him. Children, that is the way to love God with your whole heart and with your whole soul. You please God when you do good and stay away from whatever is bad.

2. Jesus said this commandment of loving God is the first and greatest commandment. Did He give us a second commandment? What is this second commandment? Jesus said it is like the first. That means, it is as great as the first. Whom else must we love besides God? Who is our neighbor according to the teaching of Jesus? Yes, every person is our neighbor. God created you and me and all people. Jesus suffered for you and me and for all people. The Holy Ghost wants to make you and me and all people holy. Did God the Father create only you and me? Did Jesus die for only you and me?

Does the Holy Ghost make only you and me holy?
No! How many people? That is right — all people.
God created all, Jesus died for all, the Holy Ghost
wants to make all holy. That is why God wants us
to love all people. He wants us all to be happy together. He wants us to make all people happy by
doing good to them. When we meet someone we
ought to think: God made this person, Jesus died
for him, and the Holy Ghost wishes to make him
holy. Then we should say to ourselves: I will do
as much good for that person as I am able.

Children, who is close to you at home? Your
parents. You must please them by obeying them
always. Besides father and mother, who else is close
to you at home? Your brothers and sisters. You
must be kind to them for the sake of God. Who
is close to you in school? Yes, your teacher and
your schoolmates. For the sake of God you must
be good to them, too. Is there anyone else close to
you? Your playmates. Do not argue, quarrel, or
fight with them during your games. Be kind to all
out of love for God.

What rule did Jesus give us by which we can
know what we must do and what we must not do
to others? Yes, children, what you want others to
do to you, you should do to them; what you do

not want others to do to you, you should not do to
them. Always act according to that golden rule because the dear God wants you to.

If you love God and your neighbor, you are good
children. You are good children if you take care to
please God and your neighbor for the sake of God.
Then God loves you, He is pleased with you and
will help you in all you do. Remember He is a
good and powerful God. Pray to Him devoutly with
all your heart, that He may help you to be always
good and kind. Ask Him to make you better and
more pious every day.

3. Jesus one day taught us a very beautiful prayer.
Your parents have said this prayer with you at
home, you have said it every day at school, and you
have often said it in church. One day a disciple
asked the dear Jesus: "Lord! teach us how to pray"
(Luke 11, 1 ff.). Jesus answered: "When you pray,
say 'Our Father Who art in heaven . . .' " etc.
(Matt. 6, 9. *Show the picture.*)

Children, God loves us as a father loves his children. From Whom have we received all things?
Body and soul? Where do we get the things we
eat? Yes, all things were made by the Father in
heaven. The dear God gave us His only Son, too.
God wants to take us to heaven if we are good.

Surely, He is our Father. He is not only my Father or your Father, but the Father of how many people? Because God is their Father, all people are His children. Now let me see if you can think. God is our Father; we are His children; then we are all . . . what relatives? That is why we pray: *Our Father*.

Children must love their father. Brothers and sisters must love one another. When you pray to God and say, "Our Father," you ought to say it with love toward God and all people. Where is God? In heaven only? Is He everywhere? But it is in heaven especially that the angels and saints honor and pray to God. That is why we say: *Who art in heaven*.

Where do we honor God in a special way on earth? God lives in our churches. That is why we honor Him in a special way there. Now think of how powerful and great God is. How easy it is for Him to give us good things and always to help us. You love God now. But you must wish to obey Him always. You must wish also that all people love Him. Can you keep good always and make other people love God by yourself alone? Who must help you? Yes, God must help you to be good, and only He can make other people good. That is why Jesus wants us to pray: *Hallowed be Thy name.* That means: "Help, dear God, that I and all people may really love You."

If we all love God, then He is pleased with us, just as a good father is pleased with His children if they are good. Where will God take our soul then after we die? Will our soul be happy in heaven? And where will God take our bodies after they have arisen from the grave on the day of judgment? Will our soul and body be happy in heaven? How long will we be happy in heaven? That is why Jesus wants us to pray: *Thy kingdom come.* That means: "Help me, dear God, and all other people to get to heaven."

But who only will get to heaven? If we wish to be good, whose will and command do we have to obey? Whose will do the angels and saints in heaven obey? Just as the angels and saints in heaven do the will of God, so all people on earth ought to do God's will. Jesus tells us to pray: *Thy will be done on earth as it is in heaven.* That means: "Dear God, help me and all people to do Your will on earth, as the angels and saints do it in heaven."

As long as we live on earth, we need food, clothes, and a house to live in. But you know, children, that everything on earth was created by God. So we must pray to God for everything that we need for our life here on earth. Then we need food for our soul, too. What food did Jesus give us for our soul? That is why Jesus wants us to pray: *Give us this day our daily bread.* That means: "Dear God, give me and all people today what we need to live, for body and soul."

If we think over what we do each day, children, we notice that we do not always act as God wants us to. Sometimes you do not pay attention in school, sometimes you do not think of the dear God when you are praying, sometimes you do not obey your good parents as you should. God is not pleased with you then. He frowns when you act like that. You know, too, that God rewards the good things you do, and that He punishes the bad things. Now, how can you keep God from punishing the bad things you have done? See, how a good child asks his father to forgive him if he has done wrong! That is the way we must ask our dear, heavenly Father to forgive us, when we have acted carelessly against His will. Jesus tells us to pray: *Forgive us our trespasses.* That means: "Forgive us our sins, dear God, forgive us the bad things we have done against You."

But let me ask you a question. Suppose a child begs his father to forgive him and then does not forgive his brother or sister when they do something against him, will that father forgive such a child? Don't you think that father will say: "Because you will not forgive your brother or sister, I will not forgive you either." In the same way, when we ask God to forgive us, He will not forgive unless we have forgiven our neighbor. Jesus teaches us to pray: *Forgive us our trespasses as we forgive those who trespass against us.* That means: "Dear God, forgive me and all people our sins. We will also forgive those who have hurt us."

God forgives those only who want to do better, those who do not want to sin any more. He forgives those who try not to do bad again, those who promise to stay away from bad companions, those who try to do only what is good. Jesus tells us to pray: *And lead us not into temptation, but deliver us from evil.* That means: "Dear God, help me and all people that we may not sin, even when we feel like doing so. Keep us free from all sin."

Now children, we will pray this beautiful "Lord's Prayer" together.

Our Father, etc. Amen.

"Amen" means the same as: Yes, I hope this from God; may my prayer be heard.

4. Your parents say another prayer right after the Our Father. This is a little prayer to the holy Mother of Jesus, the Blessed Virgin Mary. Most

of the time you say this prayer also in school and in church right after the Our Father.

Only God can make and do all things, so we pray to God alone to give us what we ask for. The holy Mother of Jesus cannot give us those things, but she can pray for us to God. God loves her so much that He will gladly help us when she asks Him.

This little prayer to the Mother of Jesus is called the Hail Mary. Children, do you still remember what the Angel Gabriel said to the holy Virgin Mary when he came from heaven to greet her? These are the words of the angel: *Hail Mary, full of grace, the Lord is with thee; blessed art thou among women.* The mother of St. John the Baptist also greeted the holy Virgin Mary some time later. These are her words: *And blessed is the fruit of thy womb, Jesus.* This is the first part of the Hail Mary: the greeting of the Angel Gabriel and of the mother of St. John the Baptist. To this we add a great favor that we wish to ask of Mary: *Holy Mary, Mother of God, pray for us sinners, now and at the hour of our death. Amen. (Show the picture.)* Now repeat with me the entire prayer. Look up at the picture as you pray.

Yes, children, the dear God loves us as a good father loves his children. As God's children, we should love Him. We should please Him. God loved us so much that He gave us His Son to save us. He loves us so much that He sends us the Holy Ghost, so that we may please Him as good children of the Catholic Church. He forgives us our sins if we ask Him and are sorry for them. He wants to make us happy forever in heaven.

God loves only what is good. We please Him when we are good. He hates what is bad. We do not please Him when we are bad. When we pray the Our Father we ask God for things that are really good for us. He is our kind Father and He will give us these things, if we pray well.

The holy Mother of Jesus, the Blessed Virgin Mary, is very powerful with God. So we greet her piously when we say the Hail Mary and ask her to pray to God for us now and especially at the hour of our death.

Religious Practice Rehearse the manner of receiving Holy Communion and the manner of going to Confession. See that all the children know the Act of Contrition well. Little children forget very easily.

Encourage the frequent reception of Holy Communion, daily Communion wherever possible.

Part Four

GENERAL REPETITION

Picture *Devices*

The Blessed Trinity

Introduction

Dear children! Today we shall once more think *Procedure* over the things I have already told you about God.

Presentation

1. *Make the large sign of the cross.* What do you say when you touch your hand to your forehead? Whose name do you mention? What do you say when you touch your breast? Whose name do you mention then? And when you go from shoulder to shoulder, what do you say? And Whose name is mentioned? How many Persons of God are named when you make the sign of the cross? What are the names of these three Divine Persons? But remember! These three Persons are only one God. (*Show the picture and let the children look at it during the lesson.*)

Who made us all and all things in heaven and on earth? What Person of God do you call the Creator? Who saved us from sin? Yes, the Second Person of

God. We call Him the Savior. As often as we make the sign of the cross, we ought to think of how the Son of God redeemed us. The Holy Ghost makes us holy. When you were baptized the Third Person of God made you holy for the first time.

2. *Pray the Apostles' Creed.* Whom do we first say we believe in? God the Father made and created all things in heaven and on earth. We call Him the Creator. Because He created everything that He willed, we call Him the almighty Creator.

Where is this dear, kind God? But He is not only in heaven. He is also on earth. In how many places? He is everywhere, even though we do not see Him. How much does God know? How does He act toward us? He is kind to us, just like a father to his children. He does so many good things for us to make us happy. We will also do many things to please Him. We will do this by always obeying Him. If we obey Him He will reward us. If we do not obey Him, He will punish us. Everything that God made must obey Him. The angels had to obey Him. Some of them did not obey. They were bad. What did God do to these bad angels? Who were the first two people God made? Did God give them any command? What was it? But they did not obey. They, too, were bad. Their sin and their badness has come upon us all. We cannot, of course, go to heaven with sin on our soul. But God promised to send Someone to save us poor people. Has God sent Him already? Who is the Savior?

Yes, we believe in Jesus Christ. The Angel Gabriel promised this Jesus to the holy Virgin Mary. Whose Son would Jesus be? When Jesus was twelve years old He said He had to speak about His Father. Whom did He mean? When Jesus was baptized, what did the voice of God the Father say about Him? We believe in Jesus Christ, the only Son of God, our Lord and Savior. The angel said the Holy Ghost would come over Mary. So we believe that Jesus was conceived by the Holy Ghost. Of whom was Jesus born — that means, who was the mother of Jesus?

To save us Jesus suffered for us. Who condemned Jesus to death? So Jesus died on the cross. Then His Body was buried. Where did His Soul go while His Body was lying in the grave? What happened on the third day? Who saw Jesus after He had arisen? Did they see Him only once? The Apostles not only saw Jesus. One of them, Thomas, touched Jesus. How long did Jesus stay on earth? Where did He go then on the fortieth day after He had arisen? In heaven Jesus has all power. He rules over the world with His Father. Will He come again as He was then? What for? He told the high priest

He was coming. The two angels said to the Apostles that He was coming.

Does Jesus come down to earth now? Where does He come? When? What is the name of the little house where Jesus lives? Where else does Jesus like to stay? Yes, in our hearts.

Jesus loved us so much. We ought to love Him in return. He is our Lord and Teacher. We ought to obey Him. He died for sin. We ought to hate sin. He showed us how to lead a good, holy life. We ought to follow Him and do as He did.

Which Person of God came upon earth after Jesus ascended into heaven? Upon whom did the Holy Ghost come? In what form did the Holy Ghost come upon the Apostles? It was the same Holy Ghost Who came upon Jesus in the form of a dove at His Baptism. The Holy Ghost makes us holy and helps us to be good. We believe in the Holy Ghost.

The Apostles then baptized many people. These people who believed and were baptized are called the Church of Jesus. Who were the different people who belonged to the Church during the time of Jesus? Who are the different people who belong to the Church of Jesus now? We must be true children of the Church of Jesus. We must believe just like the good people of long ago believed. We must do as the bishop and priests tell us. The Church of Jesus is holy. It is everywhere throughout the world. It is always the same. We must live and die as Catholics, as children of the Church of Jesus. In the Church of Jesus we have a share in all the good things that are done by all the children of the Church. That is what we mean by the Communion of Saints. We all love God. We all love our neighbor. For you know that Jesus gave us two commandments. Tell me these two commandments. How much must we love God? How do we please God? How much must we love our neighbor? Who is our neighbor?

If we commit sin and lose God's love, have we a way of getting back this love? What must we do to have God forgive us? We believe in the forgiveness of sin.

Children, listen to some more of Jesus' teaching. When our body dies, He tells us, our soul will not die. And what will happen one day to the dead body that lies in the grave? We believe in the resurrection of the body.

After Jesus calls us from the grave, our body and soul will live forever, without end. That new life that lasts forever will be happy for those who have been good, but it will be unhappy for those who have been bad and have stayed bad.

Oh, children, how beautiful these lessons of Jesus are! How happy they make us feel!

3. *Pray the Our Father.* To Whom are we speaking when we say this prayer? Who taught us this prayer? Children, we love God. We have received all things from Him. He loves us like a good father. So we must pray to Him like good children. This good Father is in heaven. He is everywhere. So we pray to Him in childlike love: Our Father Who art in heaven. God is the Father of all people. So He wants us all to love one another as brothers and sisters. We ought to pray, then, not only for ourselves, but for all people. We ought to ask God to give all people His blessings, so that we may all come to Him.

First, we ask God to help us love Him, to help us come to Him in heaven, to help us do everything He commands. We ask for these things when we pray: Hallowed be Thy Name, Thy Kingdom come, Thy Will be done on earth as it is in heaven.

Children, as long as we live on earth we need food, clothing, and a home. The thing we need most is bread. All these things come from God. So we must ask Him for all these things. And we must ask not only for ourselves but for all people. We do that when we pray: Give us this day our daily bread.

We often commit sin against God, don't we? So we must ask Him to forgive us. And God will forgive us. But Jesus tells us that we must forgive other people, too, when they do something to hurt us. So we pray: Forgive us our trespasses, as we forgive those who trespass against us.

But God will forgive our sins only if we make up our mind not to sin again. We cannot do that alone. We are poor and weak. Again we must ask the dear God to help us and all other people. In our prayer we say: Lead us not into temptation, but deliver us from evil. Amen. "Amen" means; may all I have prayed for come true.

4. *Pray the Hail Mary.* In this prayer we speak to the dear Mother of God. She is in heaven, near to God and her dear Son Jesus. Mary loves us. She prays for us. Only God, of course, can give us what we need. But Mary begs Him to hear our prayers. When we say the Hail Mary, we greet the Blessed Virgin with the same words the Angel Gabriel used, and then we ask her to pray for us now and at the hour of our death.

Oral Completion Test

1. Because God made all things in heaven and earth, we call Him . . .

2. Jesus died on the cross to . . .

3. The Holy Ghost makes us . . .

4. Because Jesus loved us so much, we ought to . . .

5. Because Jesus died for sin, we ought to . . . sin.

6. Our body and soul will live forever happy, if . . .

7. Our body and soul will live forever unhappy, if . . .

Dear children! Try to remember all these things. *Application* But above all, do the things you have learned. How good God is! He is almighty. He is always with us. He loved us so much that He gave us His only Son. His Son Jesus taught us many holy lessons. He lived a holy life. He suffered very, very much for us. The Holy Ghost wants to make us pious, good, and holy children of the Catholic Church, so that we may be happy forever with God. O God, how good You are. (*Repeat in chorus.*)

And what will we do? Yes, love the dear three Persons of God with all our heart. We will pray to God every day and always with devotion. We will be obedient to Him and never sin. Children, promise God. God help you, God bless you, children.

If time allows, we would suggest the making of *Culminating* a prayer booklet. The children might cut out pic- *Activity* tures illustrating the Apostles' Creed, the Our

Father, and the Hail Mary. These pictures would at the same time be a visual review of the principal points of doctrine. Two sheets of pictures (Prayer sheets A and B), done in sepia, can be obtained through the Archconfraternity of Christian Doctrine, Los Angeles, California, at a very low cost.

A.M.D.G.

ET

B.V.M.H.

RENEWAL OF BAPTISMAL VOWS
FOR
FIRST COMMUNION DAY

Priest: Dear children, the happy day of your First Communion has come. You are to receive Jesus in Holy Communion for the first time. The angels and the saints of heaven are happy with you. So are your parents and friends who are present in this church.

Before you receive Jesus into your hearts, I, your pastor, want you to make an act of faith before all the people here present. I want you also to renew the solemn promises that were made to God at your baptism.

Your godparents made these promises for you then. At that time you were not able to speak for yourself. But now you are old enough. May Jesus Christ, whom you are to receive into your hearts, help you! May He strengthen your faith!

(Children recite the *Apostles' Creed* and the *Our Father.*)

Priest: My dear children, do you renounce the devil?

Children: We do renounce him.

Priest: Do you renounce all his works and temptations?

Children: We do renounce them.

Priest: Do you believe in God, the Father Almighty, Creator of Heaven and earth?

Children: We do believe.

Priest: Do you believe in Jesus Christ, His only, Son, our Lord, who was born into this world and who died for us?

Children: We do believe.

Priest: Do you believe in the Holy Ghost, the Holy Catholic Church, the Communion of Saints, the forgiveness of sins, the resurrection of the body and life everlasting?

Children: We do believe.

Priest: Do you believe everything the Catholic Church believes and teaches?

Children: We do believe. For Jesus Christ founded the Catholic Church. He promised that the Church would teach only what is true. He promised to be with the Church always.

Priest: Will you always believe in the Holy Catholic Church?

Children: We will.

Priest: Will you always obey the Church?

Children: With God's help, we will live and die as good Catholics.

Priest: Then say with me (together):

O God, I thank You that I am a Catholic. / I thank You that I can believe in You, / Father, Son, and Holy Ghost. /

O God, I promise to be Your obedient child. /

I promise to be a good Catholic.

Priest: Dear children, never forget this promise. If you keep it, God will give you Heaven. He will make you happy forever.

PICTURE SUBJECTS

° Indicates a subject in the Schumacher set, size 31 by 22 inches, in colors.

* Indicates a subject in the Nelson set, size 32 by 23 inches, in colors. The pictures in these two sets are original drawings.

The subjects, to which the name of the artist is added, can be obtained from the Perry Pictures Company or Geo. P. Brown and Company, in halftone reproductions of various sizes.

°* Jesus Blessing the Children, *Hofmann* or *Plockhorst*.
°* The Creation, *Doré*.
   St. Francis and the Birds, *Giotto*.
°* Adam and Eve in Paradise.
°   Guardian Angel, *Guercino*.
   St. Michael and the Dragon, *Raphael* or *Reni*.
°* Adam and Eve Driven from Paradise.
   Jesus and the Child, *Ballheim*.
 * Jesus the Savior, *Ittenbach*.
   Mary the Maiden, *Ittenbach*.
°* Annunciation, *Hofmann* or *Bouguereau*.
°* Nativity, *Corregio*.
   Sistine Madonna, *Raphael*.
°* Adoration of the Magi, *Hofmann*.
°* Presentation, *Carpaccio*.
°* Jesus at Twelve, *Hofmann*.
°* The Home at Nazareth, *Hofmann*.
°* Jesus is Baptized, *Murillo*.
°* Jesus Cures the Sick, *Hofmann*.
°* The Good Samaritan, *Plockhorst*.
 * Jesus Feeding the Multitude, *Murillo*.

   * Jesus Raises Jairus' Daughter, *Hofmann.*
  °* Jesus Raises the Young Man of Naim, *Hofmann.*
   * Jesus Raises Lazarus, *Piombo.*
  °* Triumphal Entry into Jerusalem, *Plockhorst.*
  °* Last Supper, *Bida* or *Da Vinci.*
  °* Agony in Gethsemane, *Hofmann.*
  °* Jesus Taken Prisoner, *Hofmann.*
  ° The Scourging.
  ° The Crowning with Thorns.
   * Jesus before Pilate, *Munkacsy.*
    Ecce Homo, *Reni.*
  ° Jesus Carries His Cross, *Hofmann.*
  °* Crucifixion, *Munkacsy* or *Hofmann.*
   * Burial of Jesus, *Hofmann.*
  °* Resurrection, *Naack.*
  °* Emmaus, *Mueller.*
   * Thomas and Jesus, *Guercino.*
   * Christ Commissions His Apostles to Preach, *Schnorr.*
  °* Ascension, *Hofmann.*
  °* Descent of the Holy Ghost, *Schnorr* or *Vanderworff.*
   * St. Peter Preaching, *Fra Angelico.*
   * Marriage Feast at Cana, *Tintoretto.*
  ° Feed My Lambs, *Raphael.*
   * Child at Prayer, *Reynolds.*
  °* Jesus Teaches the Lord's Prayer.

REFERENCES

PRESENTATION AIDS

Religious Wall Pictures, Schumacher, Philip (Munich, Germany: Joseph Koesel and Frederick Pustet, 1913; New York: Frederick Pustet Company). Complete set of 60 colored pictures, 31 by 22 inches.

Bible Wall Pictures, Nelson's (New York: Thomas Nelson and Sons). Set of 282 subjects of the Old and New Testaments, in colors, 32 by 23 inches; also 188 of the above subjects, colored, in 7 by 10-inch size.

Wall Picture Rolls, Nell, Rev. George M. (Effingham, Illinois: Parish Activities Service, 1932). Four rolls of 13 pictures each: Roll 1, The Life of Christ; Roll 2, Christ Establishes His Church; Roll 3, Keeping Alive the Knowledge of the Promised Redeemer; Roll 4, The Parables of Our Lord. Colored art prints, 21 by 33 inches.

Picture Roll, Heeg, Rev. A. J., S.J. (Dayton, Ohio: The Young Catholic Messenger; Chicago: Loyola University Press, 1933). 26 colored art prints, with prayer phrases, 21 by 33 inches.

Perry Pictures (Malden, Mass.: Perry Pictures Company). Halftone reproductions of famous religious masterpieces in various sizes: 3 by $3\frac{1}{2}$, $5\frac{1}{2}$ by 8, 10 by 12 inches, for seatwork and bulletin-board display.

Brown's Famous Pictures (Beverly, Mass.: Geo. P. Brown and Company). Photographic reproductions of famous religious masterpieces in various sizes: 3 by $3\frac{1}{4}$, $5\frac{1}{2}$ by 8, etc.

310

APPLICATION — STORIES

True Stories for First Communicants, Sister of Notre Dame (London: Sands and Company; St. Louis: B. Herder Book Company, 1919).

First Communion Days, Sister of Notre Dame. (London: Sands and Company; St. Louis: B. Herder Book Company, 1920).

Ten Eager Hearts, Sister of Notre Dame (London: Sands and Company; St. Louis: B. Herder Book Company, 1924).

King of the Golden City, Loyola, Mother Mary (New York: P. J. Kenedy and Sons).

PRAYERS AND HYMNS

A Child's Happiest Moments: When Jesus Comes, Sister of Notre Dame, of Cleveland (New York: Frederick Pustet Company, 1932).

The Child on His Knees, Thayer, Mary D. (Chicago: Macmillan Company, 1928).

*Diocesan Hymnal, Books I and II, Schrembs, Most Reverend Joseph, D.D. (New York: J. Fiscner and Brother, 1928).

Welcome, Jesus, Dennerle, Rev. Geo. M. and Magdela, Sister M., S.N.D. (Milwaukee: Bruce, 1943).

St. Gregory Hymnal, Montani (Philadelphia, Pa.: St. Gregory Guild).

ACTIVITY AIDS

Art Education Through Religion, Books I, II, IV, McMunigle, Mary Gertrude (New York: Mentzer, Bush and Company, 1930).

Correlation of Art and the Mass, Reiner, Joseph, S.J., and Foster, Eunice (Chicago: Practical Drawing Company, 1931).

Practical Aids for Catholic Teachers, Aurelia, Sister Mary, O.S.F. and Kirsch, Rev. Felix M. (New York: Benziger Brothers, 1928).

Small Pictures for Pasting (Los Angeles, Calif.: Arch-confraternity of Christian Doctrine). Eighteen sheets of small sepia pictures; about 240 cuts, explaining the Catechism.

* Editor's Note: Suitable substitutions for hymns from *The Diocesan Hymnal* may be found in *The Child's Book of Hymns* by Sister Mary Editha, published in 1927 by the Sisters of Charity of Dubuque, Iowa. Reprinted by St. Augustine Academy Press in 2019.

www.ingramcontent.com/pod-product-compliance
Lightning Source LLC
Chambersburg PA
CBHW032031090426

42733CB00029B/84